WE NEED TO BUILD

FIELD NOTES FOR DIVERSE DEMOCRACY

EBOO PATEL

Beacon Press
BOSTON

BEACON PRESS
Boston, Massachusetts
www.beacon.org

Beacon Press books
are published under the auspices of
the Unitarian Universalist Association of Congregations.

25 24 23 22   8 7 6 5 4 3 2 1

This book is printed on acid-free paper that meets the uncoated paper
ANSI/NISO specifications for permanence as revised in 1992.

Text design and composition by Kim Arney

Library of Congress Cataloging-in-Publication Data is available for this title.
ISBN: 978-08070-2406-5 (hardcover) | ISBN: 978-08070-2407-2 (ebook)

For my sons:
Zayd and Khalil

I speak the pass-word primeval, I give the sign of democracy.
By God! I will accept nothing which all cannot have their
counterpart of on the same terms.

—WALT WHITMAN, from "Song of Myself"

CONTENTS

INTRODUCTION

A JOURNALIST ONCE ASKED THE CIVIL RIGHTS ICON JOHN Lewis, at that point comfortably in middle age, what it felt like to go from a protestor in the rural South to a policymaker in the nation's capital. The answer was wise and measured: when "the drama in the streets is over," the work must continue through different means in other spaces.[1]

In the case of John Lewis, the work shifted to the world of government. And as he launched his career in Congress, he came to realize that it is one thing to fight from the outside to overturn an evil regime and quite another to work from the inside to improve an imperfect nation.

Everything John Lewis did was about advancing civil rights, from his childhood preaching to chickens in rural Alabama, to his leadership role in the Student Nonviolent Coordinating Committee (SNCC), to his many terms as the representative for Georgia's Fifth Congressional District. John Lewis went from organizing demonstrations to organizing Congressional hearings; from registering his grievances through sit-ins to being the seat of power in rooms hearing out the grievances of others.

There is, no doubt, a clear through line to the work of John Lewis. Over the course of it all—from the cracked skull he suffered on the Edmund Pettus Bridge to the achievement of the Voting Rights Act, from the election of Barack Obama to the election of Donald Trump—he claims to have never despaired. He always believed that America could become a beloved community. He was proud of the progress that had been made, that indeed he had helped make. Even as a congressperson he led protests but politely quieted those in his camp who shouted "shame" upon the other side. He believed to the end that at least some of those people were potential allies who had not yet been convinced, temporary opponents who might still be won over, not permanent enemies who had to be destroyed. He had seen too much change in his own life to think differently.

As an activist in the 1960s, John Lewis marched to prevent the silencing of Black voices, the suppression of Black votes, and the erasure of Black lives. As a congressperson in the 1980s, he introduced the legislation that paved the way for the National Museum of African American History and Culture. While the spirit and values remain constant, and some of the skills (certainly speaking and organizing) transfer, there is a marked difference between being a protestor against segregation and laying the groundwork for a new and permanent Smithsonian institution. The first seeks primarily to expose structures of injustice, the second to construct a more just society.

These two dimensions of social change work can certainly go hand in hand. People are generally wary of turning away from a system that they know, bad as it might be, if they do not believe that something better can be built. And in order to trust that something better can be built, people need to have faith in the leaders doing the building.

People trusted John Lewis. He knew when to demonstrate and when to negotiate. His activism changed the space; his legislation furnished the room.

The story of Bob Moses follows much the same arc. In the 1960s, Moses played a key role in bringing down legalized racism in the Deep South. Along with John Lewis, he helped lead SNCC, served as co-director of COFO (the Council of Federated Organizations, an umbrella group of the major civil rights organizations), and was the principal organizer of Freedom Summer in Mississippi. He was a central player in the drama in the streets.

In the 1980s, while studying for his PhD at Harvard, Bob noticed that the poor Black students at his daughter's middle school were consistently tracked into lower-level math courses than the wealthy white kids. This meant that they took algebra years later. In the American education system, algebra is the gateway to higher-level educational and career pathways. Delaying algebra effectively relegates you to second-class economic status.

Bob called his initiative the Algebra Project, an institution that spread math literacy through poor Black communities. As you might imagine, this prompted some cross-eyed stares from people who admired his work in the streets. *You mean, you helped bring down Jim Crow segregation in the South, and you followed that up by . . . becoming a middle school math teacher? To top it all off, you're claiming that these things are somehow equal?*

But Bob Moses, like John Lewis, maintained that his new work was just as important as his old work. In fact, it was all part of the same work, just carried out in different sites and by different means. The protests of the civil rights movement were about political empowerment through voting. The teacher training workshops of the Algebra Project were about economic empowerment through math literacy. Both were about full citizenship in American society. When people told Moses that teaching algebra wasn't radical in the way protesting segregation was, he would quote his mentor Ella Baker on what it meant to engage in radical work: "It means facing a system that does not lend itself to your needs and devising means by which you change that system."[2]

As a young Black civil rights worker in the Deep South in the 1960s, a principal means available to Moses was protest. He would picket for hours outside local stores that refused to serve Black customers, often by himself. As founder of the Algebra Project in an America that had ended legal segregation, in part because of his efforts, Bob had a whole different set of tactics available to him. He could meet with education officials, corporate executives, local politicians, foundation presidents, and wealthy philanthropists. Precisely because his years protesting in the streets were successful, he was now able to walk through the front door of fancy buildings and negotiate at the table. In this way, he created a novel approach for engaging young people in mathematics, raised millions of dollars for his organization, spread the Algebra Project to hundreds of schools, and helped tens of thousands of poor Black kids advance along the path to economic and educational achievement.

The protests that Bob Moses helped lead in the 1960s were part of the revolution that ended an evil order of legalized segregation and discrimination. The success of that revolution paved the way for the launch of the Algebra Project, an institution that is part of the architecture of a more just new order. Bob went from demonstrating against school superintendents who supported segregation to cooperating with people in the same position to launch curriculum design workshops. That requires both an expanded set of skills and a shift in emphasis.

The life and work of Bob Moses raises a profound question: Once you have deposed people who use power for unjust ends, do you know how to take some of that power and build something better? In short, do you have what it takes to be in charge?

Being in charge means articulating a vision for what the new system will look like, offering a detailed blueprint of its various institutions, empowering and training up a group of builders, and *knowing how to build yourself*. Building something better can often be measured in clear and concrete ways. In the case of the Algebra Project, the curriculum that Bob Moses designed helped students learn better. The workshops he created for educators helped teachers teach better. His school-wide programs improved math literacy and graduation rates.

Such achievements were actually at the center of Bob Moses's vision all along. He writes: "The Civil Rights movement of the 1960s was less about challenges and protests against white power than feeling our way toward our own power and possibilities—really a series of challenges by ourselves, and our communities, to ourselves."[3]

Throughout it all, whether working with sharecroppers in Alabama or seventh graders in Chicago, Bob Moses viewed himself as an organizer in the mold of his mentor Ella Baker: "The organizer becomes a part of the community, learning from it, becoming aware of its strengths, resources, concerns, and ways of doing business. The organizer does not have the complete answer in advance . . . [but] wants to construct a solution with the community."[4]

Sometimes those solutions require you to be part of a drama in the streets; sometimes they require you to build new cultural and educational institutions.

John Lewis, Bob Moses, Ella Baker, and the other leaders of the civil rights movement of the 1960s were part of what Adam Serwer of *The Atlantic* calls founders of the Third American Republic.[5] Alexander Hamilton was a founder of the First. In Lin-Manuel Miranda's iconic telling, the early Hamilton is an all-out revolutionary. He is "young, scrappy, and hungry," fans sparks into flames, sees the ascendancy of his name and the success of the revolution as inextricably intertwined, and boldly says that he will give his life for it. The American Revolution of 1776 needed that brash spirit, both to inspire it and to win a remarkably unlikely victory against a mighty empire.

But as the show goes on, Hamilton needs to evolve. His mentor and patron George Washington reminds him that winning revolutions is easy compared to ruling well.

And so Hamilton needs to cool his hot head, to make alliances, to negotiate and compromise, to build for the long term. He writes more than he fights, builds more than he protests. Instead of throwing rocks at windows, he walks through doors and negotiates at the table in "the room where it happens."

Revolutions do not go on forever. The drama in the streets always ends and gives way to something else. Will that "something else" be better than what was in place before?

The answer to that question has everything to do with the answer to these questions: Can those who have raged against the unjust old order build and run the institutions of a new order? Can we evolve from protestors against a discriminatory regime to architects of a better system? After changing the space, can we furnish the room?

It is not an easy transition to make.

Indeed, it is harder to organize a fair trial than it is to fire up a crowd; harder to run a successful school than to tell other people that they're doing education all wrong; harder to sustain alternatives to policing that ensure public safety than it is to chant slogans in the street. And yet, every decent society needs fair trials, good schools, and public safety, and that's just the beginning of the list of institutions and structures that need to be efficiently erected and effectively run in large-scale diverse democracy.

Marc Pullins, a nonprofit leader in the neighborhood of Roseland on the far South Side of Chicago, has seen a certain type of activist come and go before. "At the end of the day, they're going back to their house . . . and they're insulated. . . . But this is our life." His neighborhood still does not have a grocery store or a dry cleaner's. Job opportunities are scarce, the schools are inadequate, and a memorial wall that honors community members lost to gun violence has over seven hundred names carved into the stone. Racism is the problem, Pullins believes; lasting institutions that improve lives are the solution.[6]

Who will build these institutions? What skills will those people require? Which visions, narratives, and symbols should serve as guides? What means should be employed? How should opponents be engaged?

This book is about those questions. It is written in the spirit of Michelle Alexander's essay "We Are Not the Resistance." The myriad outrages and offenses of the Trump administration gave rise to unprecedented opposition on virtually every important issue in American life, from income inequality to women's rights, racist police violence to immigration. Those of us who flooded the streets on any one or more of these causes came to call ourselves the resistance.

Professor Alexander celebrates that spirit but cautions that it is incomplete. She writes: "A new nation is struggling to be born, a multiracial, multiethnic, multifaith, egalitarian democracy in which every life and voice truly matters."[7] Her principal concern is that resistance is a defensive posture, geared more toward opposition than flourishing. It does not dream big enough, and it does not do enough to build new structures. Instead of the resistance, Alexander suggests that we should consider ourselves a part of the river of human freedom. Rivers, as Black freedom figures ranging from Langston Hughes to Vincent Harding have noted, have nurtured civilizations the world over from time immemorial.[8] If we are to give rise to a new civilization worthy of our highest ideals and deepest values, it will be the cultivating spirit of the river of human freedom rather than the reactive position of the resistance that will carry us there.

The goal, after all, is not a more ferocious revolution. It is a more beautiful social order.

None of this is meant as a dismissal of resistance, or its close cousins—critique, protest, opposition, and disruption. As the lawyer and activist Deepa Iyer writes, all are necessary and legitimate parts of an ecosystem of social change. But, as Iyer explains, to get from the old order to the new one requires roles like builder, weaver, and guide, in addition to frontline responder and disrupter.[9]

I am a builder—of civic institutions and of bridges. No social change ecosystem is complete without such institutions and the people who do the work to construct them. I've come to believe that it's the role that's most often taken for granted. The big protests draw the headlines, while the institutions like Highlander Folk School (now the Highlander Research and Education Center) that trained the leaders go on quietly doing their work behind the scenes—absolutely necessary and largely overlooked. But, like William Carlos Williams's red wheelbarrow, a lot depends on these institutions, and we should pay more attention to what it takes to build them.

In *A Time to Build*, Yuval Levin writes about how too many young Americans have only ever known "a national politics that feels like a debauched rampage of alienation and dysfunction—depraved and degrading, corrupting everyone who goes near it." Given this context, it is natural that some are drawn to what he calls "the demolition crews." Sadly, this means that "those who are more inclined to build are often left working without blueprints of what a more worthy alternative would look like."[10]

This book lays out those blueprints, points toward those more worthy alternatives, and offers a tool kit for building.

It is organized into three sections.

Section 1 is called "Critics and Builders." In chapter 1, I tell my own story, the racism I experienced growing up, my initiation into activism in college, and the beginnings of my personal transition from critic to builder.

Chapter 2 begins with my "You should build that" moment, the gentle challenge that an Indigenous Mayan woman named Yoland Trevino gave me at an interfaith conference in June of 1998. The rest of the chapter is the story of building the institution I constructed in response to Yoland's challenge. I draw on everything from management theory to the Grateful Dead and highlight themes that I believe are useful to builders everywhere.

For the first two decades of its existence, the organization was called Interfaith Youth Core, and often known by the acronym IFYC. In the early days, we did indeed work mostly with young people and college students. But over the years our partners expanded to include college administrators, corporate executives, government officials, and nonprofit leaders. Our ambitions have grown even broader. We believe that religious diversity is one of the great issues in American life, at the same level as, say, civil liberties and racial equity. These issues all have vital civic institutions dedicated to their protection and advancement. Think the ACLU with respect to civil liberties, or the NAACP with regard to racial equity. We at Interfaith America seek to be among the vital civic institutions engaging the great challenge and opportunity that is American religious diversity and moving the needle toward more widespread interfaith cooperation.

For clarity's sake, I will refer to the organization I run as Interfaith America throughout this book, even if the activities I describe took place while the organization was called Interfaith Youth Core.

In chapter 3, I write about friend and Interfaith America alumna the Reverend Jen Bailey, whose period of intense critique happened while she was on staff at Interfaith America and was often directed at me! She has since transformed that energy into building Faith Matters Network, an institution that has launched a range of remarkable initiatives, including the People's Supper.

In chapter 4, I zoom in on college campuses, beginning with the story of being on a specific campus during an intense student protest. I move on to consider the larger role of colleges as anchor institutions and crucibles of formation that help shape the ideals of emerging generations and teach the skills and knowledge to help make those ideals reality.

Section 2 is called "The Good Society." In this section, I zoom out and consider what it means to build a healthy diverse democracy. Chapter 5 offers a broad vision for civic life in a diverse democracy, guided by the metaphor of a potluck supper, with special attention to how a network of institutions cooperate to create a strong social infrastructure.

In chapter 6, I highlight the importance of narrative for a diverse democracy, starting with just how damaging the Trump story has been for our common life together, and reminding readers about how the story that Barack Obama narrated helped America view its diversity as the great treasure of the nation.

In chapter 7, I write about religious institutions as exemplars—at their best, they relate an inspiring narrative, they instantiate cosmic ideals in concrete programs that both serve people and nurture character, and they have stood the test of time. I illustrate this power by describing the institutions of the Aga Khan Development Network, built by my own religious community of Ismaili Muslims, and by telling the story of Ella Baker and SNCC and Bryan Stevenson and the Equal Justice Institute.

In section 3, "Considerations and Cautions," I move into a somewhat different mode and get into some of the nitty-gritty challenges about what it takes to build both an institution and a better order.

The section is organized into seventeen short chapters, things to pay attention to, not only for those who seek to struggle against unjust power but also to wield that power themselves, responsibly, in the service of building a healthy diverse democracy.

The conclusion is a letter written to my beloved sons—Khalil and Zayd, ages eleven and fourteen as I write this—offering inspiration and guidance on becoming architects of the American future.

The United States is the world's first attempt at a mass-level diverse democracy. That's one of the reasons we call this "the American experiment"—because not only was such a thing never tried before; people also considered it impossible. Part of the brilliance of Lin-Manuel Miranda's *Hamilton* is in the way it infuses the First Founding with a contemporary, diverse urban spirit, thereby giving it both a twenty-first-century style and a remarkable new nobility. I think it's a perfect expression of the possibility of this moment. The ideals of the Declaration of Independence will be realized by the very people excluded by the European settlers of the First Founding.

John Locke said, "In the beginning all the world was America."[11] Now, all the world is in America. We may be at the start of a Fourth Founding. When Stacey Abrams was asked on CNN's *State of the Union* program what Kamala Harris's election as vice president meant to her, she responded that it was proof that people of color did not only have to be agitators for specific causes or advocates for particular groups but rather could be leaders of the whole, in charge of an entire multitudinous country.[12] The first line of our manifesto for this new era should go like this: We the varied peoples of a nation struggling to be reborn are defeating the things we don't like by building the things we do.

SECTION ONE

CRITICS AND BUILDERS

CHAPTER ONE

CRITIC: A PERSONAL JOURNEY

ON THE FIRST DAY OF MY FIRST JOB OUT OF COLLEGE, I declared the institution colonialist. At least I waited until the afternoon. The institution in question was an educational program called El Cuarto Año, Spanish for "The Fourth Year." The students were between the ages of sixteen and twenty, young adults who had dropped out or been expelled from area high schools and had come to our program to prepare for the GED. We called it a school, but really it was just a handful of modest rooms on the third floor of a large social services organization called The Association House, located in the rapidly gentrifying neighborhood of Wicker Park on the near Northwest Side of Chicago.

I suppose my declaration was accurate, in so far as every institution in a society founded on slavery and genocide is colonialist. But the reason for my announcement had far more to do with my own psychology than it did with the politics of the school. To put it simply, I was scared. I had been hired to teach urban Black and Hispanic high school dropouts and help them get their GEDs. At that time, I had never met an urban minority high school dropout. I had never taught school before, or taught anything really. And I didn't have the faintest clue about the GED; I don't think I'd ever even heard of it before applying for the job.

If you're wondering how I'd landed a faculty position given the combination of my paper-thin résumé and inflated sense of self, please know that I'd actually been hired as an AmeriCorps volunteer, meant to serve as needed and learn on the job. But as luck would have it, one of the recently hired teachers had declined the job offer at the last minute, and the administration didn't have much choice; there I was, front and center, green but eager.

You can imagine how scared and disoriented I was on that first day. I was a week away from facing a room full of students and I'd have to stand up in front of a class and lead a lesson. Then I would have to give them an assignment to see if they'd retained the content, and then I'd have to evaluate them based on a rubric. I needed to do this day after day for several months. After that, the students would take a test that would determine whether they would get a $2 an hour raise at work, which was the reason, according to the applications they had filled out, that many of them had returned to school in the first place.

It didn't take me long to recognize that the other teachers had far more classroom experience than me, and more life experience too. I was twenty at the time, barely older than our students. As an undergraduate at the University of Illinois, I was accustomed to being recognized. I was the smart one in classes, the very visible leader of various activist causes and student groups. I clearly wasn't going to get recognized in this group by my expert pedagogy or my knowledge of the student population. I was petrified of being found out. And so I reached for something that would both distinguish me and cause diversion: I played the role of radical critic.

Remarkably, the other teachers absorbed what I said in a spirit of calm. Their basic attitude was, "Yep, we've read the same theorists you have. Happy to name-check them along with you if you'd like. But we've got something more immediate to do here—figure out a way to teach these students as best we can. We'll help you, but you've got to be willing to learn."

That is exactly what happened over the course of that year. I stopped playing the role of revolutionary and instead allowed myself to be mentored by expert teachers and community builders. The best advice I got about education and empowerment was from the Mexican American math teacher, Joel, who told me: "Give these students what you take for granted—the core academic skills necessary for navigating the world. They'll make their own decisions about politics. Trust me, they don't lack for evidence when it comes to the problem of structural racism."

I was lucky. My big mouth had placed me in a hard spot; my colleagues gave me a soft landing.

My initiation into activism took place at the hands of a Marxist political science professor at the University of Illinois. He assigned us Noam Chomsky and Howard Zinn, brought in guest speakers who had violently protested the Vietnam War, and gave us class credit for going to campus demonstrations against the university's racist mascot, Chief Illiniwek. Discussions revolved around the various injustices we had all been witness to, our professor listening intently as we groped our way toward political consciousness. He engaged our minds and encouraged our rage.

One day, he asked me about the racism I had experienced as a child. I don't think any teacher had ever asked me that before. I wouldn't have described myself as especially given to anger before coming to college. But once the question was posed, the memories came pouring out. It turns out that I didn't have to dig very deep to find my rage.

I grew up as a brown kid in the white western suburbs of Chicago in the 1980s. When I was ten years old and my brother nine, we went trick-or-treating on Halloween in our leafy little subdivision called the Glen Ellyn Woods. We arrived at a house right as the Clayton kids got there. They were the same ages as us and were white, like about 90 percent of the other kids in the area. "Trick or treat," we said to the nice old woman who opened the door. She smiled and handed us our candy, then she asked, sweetly and innocently, "Are you all trick-or-treating together?" The older Clayton kid looked at my brother and me, made a face like he smelled spoiled milk, and said: "Are you kidding? We're not with them." Then the Clayton kids laughed and ran to the next house. The old woman looked at my brother and me like she didn't quite understand. But my brother and me, we just trudged home and didn't say a word to each other. We both knew exactly what had happened.

Sometimes the racism was more overt. I remember being twelve years old and a student at Glen Crest Middle School. The class was social studies, the unit was on India, and the teacher said that women in India wear dots on their heads. "I don't really know why they do it," he remarked, and added, "I think it looks silly." I don't really think the teacher meant anything malicious by that, but even still, "dot-head" became a favorite and frequently deployed slur amongst the kids in the class. They started taking cheap felt-tip pens and drawing dots on their foreheads and saying, "Hey, look, I'm Eboo's mom." And then they let loose a string of gibberish in what they took to be an Indian accent. My mom doesn't have an Indian accent, and she doesn't have a dot on her forehead. We're Muslim, not Hindu. Some of the kids knew this because they had been over to my house and eaten my mom's food. Still, they drew dots on their foreheads, mimicked an Indian accent, and mocked my mom.

And sometimes the racism just snuck up on you. I remember being fourteen years old, visiting my uncle in suburban Los Angeles, and helping out at his Subway sandwich store. My parents owned Subways too, so I was experienced behind the counter. A customer walked in and I politely asked what kind of sandwich he wanted. "I want a Cold Cut Combo," he said. He paused for effect, and then continued: "But you're not making any sandwiches for me—she is." He pointed to the woman I was working with, a woman who was older than me but less experienced as a Subway employee. "My family owns Subways back in Chicago," I said. "I've been making sandwiches for a while now. I can make it." The customer took two steps toward me and said, "You're not making my sandwich—she is. And I'm not saying it again." I didn't argue; I just stepped back. It took me a minute to realize what had happened. It wasn't my age that the customer didn't like.

He was white; the woman I was working with was white. He didn't want someone with brown skin touching his food.

These kinds of things happened repeatedly but irregularly—four or five times one month, none the next. The vast majority of customers who I served at Subway were perfectly polite, most of what my teachers said was educational and encouraging, but I always had it in the back of my mind that a white customer might demand to be served by a white employee, or that a teacher might make an off-hand comment that set off a spate of casual racism. Even after the dothead phase in junior high passed, I found myself highly anxious when those kids came over to my house. Were they studying how my mom talked and dressed so they could bully me about her at school? Was I being a traitor to my family by having kids who made fun of our heritage over to my house? Shouldn't I just be grateful that I had friends (sort of friends, I guess) at all? There were other brown kids at school who were getting bullied far worse than I was, and no one would ever go over to *their* houses. That included me. To be friends with *those* brown kids would be to highlight that I was also a brown kid, rather than a white kid in brown skin.

For the longest time, I did not call any of this racism. Racism, I had learned in high school, meant slavery and segregation. There were a few paragraphs in our history book about it, and in literature class we read *To Kill a Mockingbird* and some poems by Langston Hughes. Nobody was whipping me while I picked cotton, or making me eat my food in a separate room, or framing me in a criminal trial, so why would I even think of applying the term "racism" to what I was going through? I didn't have either the language or the sociological categories to help me make sense of my experience.

My first recollection of hearing the phrase "white supremacy" in college was in my Sociology 100 course. The images of men wearing white sheets and burning crosses came to mind, and I figured my professor was referring to ancient history. But she continued: "White supremacy is the assumption that the cultural patterns associated with white people—from clothes to language to aesthetic preferences to family structure—are normal, and the patterns associated with people of color are inferior."

Wait, didn't that basically describe, like, *my entire life*? Feeling strange about my grandmother's clothes, about my grandmother's cooking, about the fact that my grandmother even lived with us? You mean there was a phrase for my feeling that was considered academic, that I could read about and write papers on? It turns out that there was a whole language for this, with phrases like "institutionalized racism" and "structures of oppression." There were influential theories, indeed entire academic fields, built on those ideas.

I started at the University of Illinois in 1993, a time when such theories were no longer relegated to specialty graduate seminars but rather were taught on the first day of introductory courses. I, for one, could not get enough. The theory of white supremacy helped me see my entire life in a different light. I remembered the presentation my dad had given at a conference of South Asian businesspeople in Chicago. Someone asked him why he had decided to buy a Subway sandwich store instead of starting an independent shop. "Which white people do you know are going to buy sandwiches from a brown guy born in India named Sadruddin?" he responded. "A recognizable franchise covers your dark skin and ethnic name. It helps you hide."

At the time the comment had struck me as perfectly logical and entirely unremarkable. My dad had simply spoken a basic truth of social life, the equivalent of noting that gravity pulls you down. I remember most of the audience nodding along. But in light of critical race theory, I interpreted the moment differently: it was a bullet fired from the gun of American racism.

I took the eyes of critical race theory into the world and saw the arsenal of racism everywhere. In the names of sports teams like the Cleveland Indians and the Atlanta Braves. In the terrible disparities between Black and white, from prison sentencing to school quality. In the casual language used by frat boys as they passed me on the quad.

Soon, I couldn't see much else. Racism was everywhere, in every-thing. It was my job to call it out, beat it down, and give it a violent death in front of a crowd.

Critical race theory had gone from a useful additional perspective to the only acceptable answer to every possible question; an interest-ing and creative critique had somehow morphed into the controlling paradigm.

For me, critical race theory wasn't just about removing the bullets from the gun of the oppressor; it was also about loading my own. It was a weapon I fired every chance I got.

When I was in my second year as a student at the University of Illinois, fully in the swing of protest activism, I heard a rumor that my beloved Unit One Living-Learning program, where many of the most progressive courses at the University of Illinois were held, faced a pos-sible $10,000 budget cut. I cocked my gun and asked around about who had ultimate authority for budgets at the university. Someone told me it was the provost.

After every class, for the next week, I called that office. Three, four, five times a day, I rang the number. I told his assistant my name and that I wanted to talk to the provost about the budget cut that I was taking highly personally. She said she was unaware of any such budget cut but she'd pass along the message. The fifth time I called, she interrupted me when I said my name. "I know who you are," she said icily. By the tenth time she'd stopped telling me that she would pass the message along. On the fifteenth or sixteenth attempt, she finally said, "He's got five minutes, make the most of it," and put me through.

I launched in before he got out the word "Hello."

"How dare you consider cutting the Unit One budget," I shouted from the courtesy phone in the student union. "Are you afraid of the activist culture there? Concerned that we host speakers who talk about institutionalized racism and structures of inequality? We are the students who are going to change the world; we won't let you take our program away from us." I could feel people staring at me as they walked by.

"Hold on, hold on, HOLD ON," came the voice on the other end of the phone. *"What are you talking about?"* It was a voice that sounded like it was accustomed to being in charge. A white man's voice. That just enraged me further.

"We *know* you are considering a $10,000 cut to the Unit One budget," I yelled. Did this guy think he was dealing with some clueless fraternity dude?

"Listen," the provost said, a combination of amusement and exasperation in his voice, "I deal with a budget in the hundreds of millions of dollars. Do you really think $10,000 decisions make it to my desk? Can you remind me what Unit One even is?"

It made perfect sense when he put it like that, such good sense in fact that I wish I had thought of simply asking someone who might be making the budget decision on the $10,000 cut rather than jumping straight to berating the provost.

I hung up the phone, my righteousness slowly melting into embarrassment.

I was so intent on critiquing the system that I hadn't paused along the way to figure out how it actually worked.

My criticism wasn't just reserved for people in positions of authority.

A friend of mine started a South Asian Cultural Association and invited me to attend the first meeting. I didn't have much to do that night, so I went. As people were mingling and getting to know one another, a little voice inside me went berserk. I stood up and gathered people around. The friend who had invited me must have been shocked—I'd been a last-minute yes to this meeting, and now I was calling it to order? I proceeded to make a speech that went something like this: "To have any integrity at all," I thundered, "this group must take a stand against colonialism." And then I added, after a dramatic pause, "In all its forms."

There were several students in the room *who had recently emi-grated from South Asia*. It must have seemed strange to them to watch me give the opening speech about how to define a group about South Asian culture. I was a little afraid that one of them might stand up and say thank you very much but would the loud American please sit down. Instead, my speech only caused them to look a bit confused and lean back. I was relieved when another student activist loudly agreed with me. She used the opportunity to speak about her research in the area of postcolonial theory and said she also saw this group as a way to put theory into practice. I wanted to be on vanguard, but I didn't want to be alone. My friend the organizer shot me a nonplussed look, but I was too proud of my speech to pay him much mind. What I do remember is overhearing a graduate student from Hyderabad say to the person next to him, "I was only coming to make new friends who share my culture. This campus is very lonely. I don't know if I want all of this," he continued, motioning my way.

I never went back to another meeting. Being South Asian matters to me, but it's not something I typically organize around, and I had too much else on my plate at that time to help start a student group. Something else was going on for me that night. I was trying out a persona, a mode of expression, a style of identity performance. After deciding the shirt didn't fit, I gave it up.

My biggest regret is the experience of that student from Hyder-abad. As I said, I never went back to another meeting of that club, so I don't know if he ever went back either. If my grandstanding had some-how given him the wrong impression of a group that he had much more need for and right to than I had, and he had felt discouraged from returning because I had felt the need to make a self-righteous speech, I should be charged with a kind of activist crime. But at the time, that's how I thought social change happened: you plant your flag in the most radical territory imaginable, get out your bullhorn, and loudly demand that people cross the line and join your side.

In my final semester at the University of Illinois, I did an independent study specifically on critical race and gender theory with an African American female professor of theater and education. We focused on Paulo Freire, bell hooks, and Augusto Boal. Even though many of the theorists we read had devised strategies of constructive change, and my professor frequently attempted to steer our conversations in that direction, I only wanted to talk about the parts that emphasized what was wrong with the world.

Toward the end of the semester my professor invited me to attend a dress rehearsal of a play she had written with her graduate students. Children are one of the most oppressed groups in our society, she told me, and the play was an experiment at a type of theater that put kids at the center.

I was excited about attending, eager to demonstrate how much I had learned in our critical theory independent study. I sat in the audience and made notes throughout the performance, highlighting all the ways that the play itself was a tool of oppression. I could barely wait until it was over. My list was long and impressive.

I was the first person to stand during the talk-back session. My professor smiled broadly when she saw me, thrilled that I had accepted her invitation to attend. I launched into my list, and the smile disappeared. I began by critiquing a scene where one of the kids, after a fight with a parent, retreated to his own room to reflect on his thoughts and feelings. The intention was to show the child's perspective to an audience that might instinctively identify with the adult, but I was reading the scene from the perspective of the oppressed, so I scolded my professor and her graduate students—in front of the entire audience—for racism and classism for the crime of writing a character that had his own room. "What about all the families where kids don't have their own rooms? Or the families that don't have houses? Don't you realize that your play is only further oppressing them?"

The cast stared at me in disbelief. There were no more questions or comments from the audience. An uncomfortable silence blanketed the room. My critique had been the first word, and the last.

I had hoped my professor would be proud of me. After all, I had done what we had discussed in our independent study—criticize. So the email she sent me came as a total surprise.

Her students, she wrote, had worked so hard on the play and were deeply hurt by my comments. She was hurt too. Why hadn't I offered constructive suggestions, she wondered? Why had I been so merciless with people who had given their all to create something positive?

She closed with this: "Since you were disappointed with the play that these students wrote, you should try your hand at creating something better. It is always harder to create than it is to criticize."

I sat with that email for a long time. My critical theory professor, perhaps inadvertently, was teaching me the limits of critical theory. Simply put, looking for the bad in everything means that you ignore the good, and you absolve yourself of any responsibility for building things that are better. Moreover, whenever human beings are involved in a situation (aren't they always), they get hurt in the process. What's the point of hurting people who are doing their best to make concrete improvements to the world, however imperfect?

I was a week away from graduating, and while I wasn't exactly sure what the next phase of my life would hold, I had a sneaking suspicion that the time when my main job was to write papers that critiqued the system and receive A's from professors as a result was over.

And I thought a lot about my professor's comment on the importance of creating rather than condemning. I knew that there was a role for people who sit in the audience and criticize the show. But I was increasingly realizing that was not who I wanted to be. I wanted to be the person putting something on the stage.

CHAPTER TWO

BUILDER, CREATING INTERFAITH AMERICA

"YOU SHOULD BUILD THAT."

I was at an interfaith conference, the United Religions Initiative global summit at Stanford University. It was two years after I graduated from college and I was looking for a way to be involved in social change without being consumed by rage.

My college activism had been nurtured in circles of anger. I would lead protests saying, "Tools can be weapons if you hold them right," paraphrasing the Ani DiFranco lyric.[1] I often followed it up with the famous line from Audre Lorde: "The master's tools will never dismantle the master's house."[2]

Dismantling systems was my entire focus. I remember a classroom conversation with a radical professor about where all of our fervent protest and critique was leading. What was the endgame? The professor spoke: "When we raise our voices in opposition, we are pushing against the system. Even now, as we discuss these things, the system is bending. And one day, it will bend so far that it will break."

I nodded my head in pious agreement. At the time, it almost sounded romantic. *We enlightened few could take down an oppressive system with our brilliant critique and forceful protest.*

There was no talk about what better system might replace the one we destroyed. And no one mentioned the knowledge or skills we might need to build it.

Toward the end of my time in college and certainly in the months immediately following, I had come to the slow realization that the burning-down-oppressive-structures-with-my-rage approach wasn't for me. For sure, a controlled burn powered by righteous anger can be necessary for regeneration, but it is not the role I want to play. I don't like alienating people. I don't like being angry. There was no glorious new birth after my various scorched-earth raids, just an awful lot of burned ground and damaged relationships. The problem with rage, as Howard Thurman pointed out, is that it tends to destroy more than the intended target.[3]

I was slowly shifting to the approach advocated by the Black queer Episcopal priest Reverend Pauli Murray: "I intend to destroy segregation by positive and embracing methods. When my brothers try to draw a circle to exclude me, I shall draw a larger circle to include them."[4]

Pauli Murray's circle was wide enough to include even the hateful and the vile. She was one of the students who argued that the segregationist governor of Alabama, George Wallace, should be allowed to speak at Yale and expressed hope that the love-based activism he would encounter on campus might change him.

Could love-based activism really change the world? By the end of my college years, I was reading the work of a lot of serious people who deeply believed that it could and had given their lives to the cause: John Lewis, Martin Luther King Jr., Badshah Khan, Mahatma Gandhi, Mother Teresa, Dorothy Day, the Dalai Lama, Abraham Joshua Heschel, Thich Nhat Hanh, and many more. It didn't take long for me to recognize that these were all people of deep religious conviction, and from a range of different faiths. I found myself especially inspired by stories of these figures learning from each other's religions and working together across their diverse faiths. I wanted to tap into that energy, so I started going to interfaith events.

And that is how I wound up at that conference at Stanford. I had gone looking for heroes from different traditions creating urgent movements, the contemporary version of Pauli Murray and Badshah Khan. I had found mostly older white Christian theologians pontificating from panels. Some of my college-era activist anger must have welled up in me, because at one point during the event I stood up from the floor and shouted: "Where's the diversity? There's no action here, no young people, no edge. *You people are killing me, you are so boring.*"

And that's when the moment happened. An Indigenous Mayan woman named Yoland Trevino approached me after my explosion. "I think you're right," she said. She motioned to the conference participants, now starting to make their way to the lunch buffet. "Interfaith work these days *is* largely old, white, male, Christian leaders talking. Sounds like you have a vision for something different—an interfaith movement full of young people and focused on social action. That's powerful. *You should build that.*"

The sculptor, said Michelangelo, sees an angel hiding in the stone and does the work of releasing it. The mentor sees a constructive vision in the rage-filled critique and invites the change agent to build it. That's the role that Yoland Trevino played for me in that moment.

The email from my theater professor in college was one of the first times I had been challenged to create rather than criticize. I had experienced it as a gentle nudge, as if my professor had said: This is a path you should consider.

In contrast, I felt like Yoland Trevino had grabbed me by the scruff of my neck. Strange as it may sound, I had felt it forcefully precisely because she had spoken so graciously. My standard tone when I was in activist mode was a mixture of flippancy and scorn, a cocktail that basically conveyed, "You idiots in charge couldn't find a tree if you were looking at a forest."

Yoland had taken an entirely different approach. She'd essentially said to me: I'm impressed by how clearly you see things. Please build what you see—it would make the world so much better. The message I took away was, if it's as easy as I seem to be saying to build things, then I should be able to do it.

Turns out that building things is not quite that easy, but it is worth it.

This chapter is about my twenty-year journey of responding to Yoland's challenge by building the institution of Interfaith America, and about the lessons I have learned along the way. Over those two decades, I have found myself constructing more than critiquing and collaborating more than opposing. My work has been characterized more by an outstretched hand rather than a raised fist. I suppose I look at those lines by Audre Lorde and Ani DiFranco about tools and weapons and houses differently now. Why would I walk through the world looking to hurt someone rather than to build something? Why would I spend energy tearing houses down rather than building better structures up? After all, no one wants an environment in which wounding people and destroying things becomes the norm.

In fact, when I think back on the times I flung jags of flippancy and scorn at those trying to make small concrete improvements to an imperfect world, I am deeply ashamed.

Building something is much different than starting something. I launched a variety of activist initiatives in college; some lasted for a semester, some for a year. It hadn't occurred to me to put energy into sustaining them. I did what felt most important in the moment, and then I moved on.

Truth be told, my frame of mind hadn't yet shifted when I took Yoland Trevino up on her challenge. I figured I'd run an interfaith action project or two and then go on to something else. But the more deeply I got into interfaith work, the more I found myself influenced by traditions that prioritized the sustainable over the ephemeral.

"The Church thinks in centuries, not in daily news cycles," a Jesuit priest once told me.

"If the final hour reaches upon you while there is a sapling in your hand, plant it," said the Prophet Muhammad in a famous hadith.[5]

Institutions, built right, have the chance to influence nations and generations. In *A Time to Build*, Yuval Levin refers to institutions as "the durable forms of our common life. They are the frameworks and structures of what we do together . . . The institution organizes its people into a particular form moved by a purpose, characterized by a structure, defined by an ideal, and capable of certain functions."

The definition of a good society, in my view, is a network of good institutions working together. I mean "good" in terms of both ideals and effectiveness.

We Americans actually have a glorious tradition of this kind of institution building. Alexis de Tocqueville, the great nineteenth-century French observer of the United States, wrote that the "mother science" of America was "the art of association." As Tocqueville is often considered amongst the original theorists of American civic life, he is worth quoting at length on this matter. "Americans use associations to give fetes, to found seminaries, to build inns, to raise churches, to distribute books, to send missionaries to the antipodes; in this manner they create hospitals, prisons, schools. . . . Everywhere that, at the head of a new undertaking, you see the government in France and a great lord in England, count on it that you will perceive an association in the United States."[6]

My contribution to the civic infrastructure of American society, a contribution that I hope inches our society along the path of being good, is Interfaith America. At the twenty-year mark, it is an institution with fifty professional staff and a ten-million-dollar budget. I will spare you a detailed description of each brick that has gone into making the structure. What follows instead are themes and stories from the Interfaith America experience that I believe translate into useful lessons for institution builders everywhere.

THE RESTAURANT ANALOGY

"What does the world look like if you are successful?"

I admit the question made me squirm a bit. It was December of 2002 and I was at the Metropolitan Club at the Sears (now Willis) Tower, sitting across from a man named Ron Kinnamon. He had called the Interfaith America office out of the blue and said he'd been reading some of the news articles about the organization I was trying to start, and he wanted to take me to lunch. We exchanged pleasantries over the soup, and then Ron got down to business in his gentle-but-probing way.

"Tell me about the vision. Tell me about how an observer would know if you achieved it."

I talked about the racism I'd experienced as a child and the positive inspiration I had found in Islam, stories that journalists in that post–9/11 era loved writing about. I described Interfaith America's next project down to the level of nitty-gritty detail that foundation program officers frequently demanded. I even gushed about the fact that we'd gotten our first intern from the University of Chicago School of Social Service Administration.

I knew that none of it came close to answering the question of how the world would be different if Interfaith America succeeded. Ron knew it too. But he didn't give up on me. Instead, he leaned forward and said, "I think your organization could have a big impact over the long term. America has no clue how to be a truly religiously diverse democracy. Your organization can show us. But you need to be able to do more than talk about your personal story and run random projects. To fulfill your potential, you are going to need to be able to articulate a broader vision and build an institution capable of running a network of programs that make that vision a reality."

He used a billiards analogy. "Right now, you're playing pool ball by ball. That's how beginners do it. Pros are always thinking many plays ahead. It's not about hitting the next shot; it's about setting up the whole table."

Earlier in the meal, Ron and I had connected over our experiences at the YMCA. Ron had spent fifty years working for the Y and had retired as the number-three person in the national office. I had spent virtually every day of my childhood at the B. R. Ryall Y in Glen Ellyn, from after-school care to Friday night basketball, day camp to Leaders School. The Y had shaped my life, and Ron had shaped the strategy of the Y.

"Most people think about the Y through the particular program they experience," he said. "Maybe it's camping, maybe it's swim team. But those of us in leadership positions think about the *larger vision* of the Y, which is about connecting all people to their potential, purpose, and each other. Running effective programs is how we accomplish the vision. There are some things that are signature programs—overnight camps and swim instruction, for example. But there are other things that have been developed to meet the needs of different eras and diverse communities. We started after-school care when women went to work in large numbers in the 1970s and 1980s because it was a program that got the world closer to the deeper purpose. If our identity was only tied to swim and gym and camp, we would never have started after-school care. And if we didn't run our signature programs well, the public wouldn't have trusted us enough to participate in major new initiatives."

It all felt so simple and so revelatory at the same time. In those first years at Interfaith America, I'd been so consumed by the mechanics of starting an organization—running projects, recruiting participants, hiring staff, moving into a proper office, finding the next foundation grant, putting together a board, getting media attention—that I hadn't taken time to figure out an overarching vision or strategy. Success to me was a repeat cycle of getting a grant, running a project, making a speech, and having an article appear in the paper.

Maybe it's because we were at lunch that a restaurant analogy came to mind. At that point in my leadership of Interfaith America, I thought of myself as the chef-owner of a single restaurant. I had to know the menu inside and out, make sure the food was properly prepped, position the cooks at the right stations, and gear up to get through the lunch rush. Ron wanted me to have all the skills of a chef but to actually think of myself as the restaurateur. The person who came up with the concept, thought through the design of the space, figured out how to source the ingredients, created a novel cuisine, trained chefs and line cooks, paid attention to the customer experience, and, most of all, *considered how the entire enterprise changed how people thought about the relationship between the natural environment, food, and their bodies.*

I was running Interfaith America as a quick lunch spot. Ron thought it could be Chez Panisse.

I think one of the reasons this was new for me is because, up until that point, I'd spent most of my life as a participant in programs other people designed. To continue the analogy, I was a diner at someone else's restaurant, and I had become adept at critiquing the food and the service. By starting Interfaith America, I'd had the gumption to effectively say, "Let me into the kitchen. I've got an idea for some dishes that are tastier than what you've got on the menu, and I'm certain they would attract a different crowd." But that was as far as I'd gotten.

Ron was inviting me to think institutionally, which is to say several levels up from any individual program.

It took years, but we finally came up with the answer to Ron's question of what the nation looks like when we achieve our vision at Interfaith America. Simply put, the purpose of the organization Interfaith America is to build the *nation* Interfaith America. In other words, we hope to advance the national narrative beyond "Judeo-Christian" to a wider embrace of the country's religious diversity. We will know we have achieved Interfaith America when it is simply commonplace for cities across the country to have days of interfaith service; when there is an established scholarly field called interfaith studies that certifies tens of thousands of people every year who have the knowledge base and skill set of interfaith leadership; when companies, schools, hospitals, and civil society organizations hire interfaith leaders because they recognize the significance of proactively engaging the religious diversity within their organizations; when houses of worship regularly have partnerships across faith lines; when people across traditions can readily articulate the theology or ethic of interfaith cooperation of their own community; when organizations across sectors view it as standard operating procedure to have interfaith strategic plans; when teaching the history of religious diversity in the United States is a robust part of every high school American history course. Most importantly, when religious diversity is understood as a powerful and visible asset that ought to be engaged positively and proactively rather than a dynamic that is either invisible or a threat.

Ron Kinnamon, may he rest in peace and power, would be pleased.

SIGNATURE PROGRAMS
AND PATTERNS OF ACTIVITY

World wars and global pandemics notwithstanding, Harvard University will open in fall 2022, welcoming thousands of young people into classrooms to be taught by faculty who are widely recognized in their particular academic field. Harvard has been doing this for four hundred years and will likely be doing it for four hundred more. Older universities—Al Azhar, Oxford, Bologna—have been doing some version of the same even longer.

This is so common that we simply take it for granted. But in-person classes taught by expert faculty to classrooms of young people in a designed physical environment is a signature program, part of a pattern of activity at one of the most impressive civic institutions human beings have ever built: the university. There are other signature programs that are part of the pattern of activity at these institutions: the editing of scholarly journals, scientific research conducted in laboratories, the collecting and maintaining of academic materials in libraries. And this is just the beginning. There are athletic teams, social clubs, student groups, ceremonial activities like commencement, publications like the *Harvard Crimson*.

A *signature program* is something that a particular institution is especially good at doing and has come to define the institution, both to itself and in the mind of the public. A *pattern of activity* is the set of signature programs that an institution expects itself, and is expected by the public, to do, year over year, in a roughly routinized manner. A university is a collection of signature programs that has been shaped into a year-over-year pattern of activity. If you think about it, so is a museum, a theater, and a concert hall. The Field Museum will have permanent exhibits, Steppenwolf Theatre will have a season of plays, Symphony Center will put on a series of classical music concerts. You can set your calendar to it—many people do.

Each of these civic institutions will also take on special initiatives, depending on the proclivities of its leadership, the interests of its public, and the availability of funding. The Field Museum will have rotating exhibits and occasional lectures. Harvard will run different research and public engagement projects. Steppenwolf might hold a concert or a poetry reading. When things go particularly well, special initiatives become signature programs. A number of museums in Chicago experimented with weekly music in the courtyard programs during the summer. It turned out that the deck at the Museum of Contemporary Art was a wonderful place to play and listen to jazz, and now the MCA has made it a signature program, part of its pattern of activities. It has gotten better at everything, from sound quality to food service, and even found ways to connect the music outside with the art inside. Furthermore, the MCA's audience expects to see the schedule of musicians who will play on the deck once the weather turns warm.

When we first started, I thought of Interfaith America as an idea expressed in a couple of projects. The idea was that young people who oriented around religion differently should engage positively and proactively, working together on common ground projects and finding enriching ways to discuss differences. The projects we ran ranged from the youth program at the Parliament of the World's Religions in South Africa in 1999 to an interfaith service project with Habitat for Humanity in January 2001 to a Chicago Youth Council. But these were entirely opportunistic; we waited to see what another institution was doing, we added our car to the train, and we went along for a ride whose destination was determined by someone else.

Once we were able to start running a collection of projects—a Chicago Youth Council, plus the Days of Interfaith Youth Service, plus the occasional National Conference, plus produce an Interfaith Best Practices Toolkit—I began to think of Interfaith America as an organization. But even then, these were year to year, dependent on temporary grants and often run by young staff who would be with the organization for a year or two between finishing college and heading off to graduate school.

It wasn't until Interfaith America reached the point of having signature programs and established patterns of activity that I felt we had arrived in the civic institution category. Getting there was anything but a straightforward journey.

Every once in a while, I'll run across an old brochure for an Interfaith America activity that lasted for a year or two and commence a long stroll down memory lane. In 2007, for example, we launched an Interfaith Fellows program on college campuses, selecting twenty exceptional students from a competitive pool of undergraduates who applied to be bridge builders across religious differences on campus. The program only lasted a couple of years. It was expensive and not scalable. But in that time, we figured out how to run an application process that included both the student applicant and a staff/faculty mentor; develop and implement an intensive in-person training for young leaders; and get a sense of what effective student-led interfaith work on campus could look like.

After making the difficult decision to sunset that program, we asked ourselves if we could take the original vision (students on campus trained and dedicated to running interfaith programs) and do it in a more cost-effective and scaled way. What if we created an Interfaith Leadership Institute (ILI) where we trained hundreds of students in the methods we had developed through the Fellows program? We thought of it as an experiment, a special initiative, and launched. The first ILI was in 2010 at Georgetown and was wildly successful.

Ten years later, the ILI is an Interfaith America signature program, a centerpiece of our pattern of activities. Every August, hundreds of campuses send student delegations to Chicago to get inspired and trained in interfaith bridge building skills. It is written in their calendars in ink. Every year, Interfaith America staff evaluates the Institute and makes improvements to the program for the following year. Some of the improvements we made turned out to not really be improvements—like doing regional ILIs based on host institutions and local funders. That lasted for a couple of years before we realized it was too cumbersome to maintain. Other improvements, like establishing different tracks for different levels of interfaith expertise, have stood the test of time.

MONEY AND STRATEGY

Amongst the many nuggets of wisdom that Ron Kinnamon shared with me at that first lunch at the Metropolitan Club was this: "To be an effective institutional leader, you can't be afraid of money, but you can't be a fool for it either." People build civic institutions for all kinds of reasons: they really want to solve a particular social problem, they believe deeply in a particular program, they care about a certain population of people. Nobody has ever started a civic institution because they love to raise money. That includes me. But over the years, it's become something I enjoy rather than dread. A lot of this has to do with my friendship with Jennifer Hoos Rothberg and David Einhorn of the Einhorn Collaborative (known once as the Einhorn Family Charitable Trust). Look back on the history of any long-lasting and successful institution and there was probably a deep partnership between the leader of that institution and a key funder during a crucial period. Geoffrey Canada had Stanley Druckenmiller when he was transitioning the Rheedlen Centers into the much more ambitious Harlem Children's Zone.[7] At Interfaith America, I had Jenn and David.

The Einhorn Collaborative was just getting started and it had a deceptively simple vision and a distinctive strategy. The vision was a world where everyone got along better. The strategy was to find organizations that Jenn and David considered field leaders in sectors that could make meaningful change toward their mission and invest big. Like seven to eight figures big.

When it comes to the world of philanthropy, this is as rare as an eighty-degree day during a Chicago winter. Many funders give you part of what you say you need to run a single project and then weigh the grant down with all sorts of burdensome rules and reporting requirements. To top it off, grants are typically no more than three years and, when you go back for a renewal, you often discover that the funder has gone through a strategic plan and has a new set of priorities. It's possible to run special initiatives this way, but it's impossible to build an institution, even with multiple such grants.

I learned this the hard way. By 2008, Interfaith America had a $2.5 million budget, twenty-five staff, and absolutely zero strategic coherence. I had followed the first part of Ron's dictum—to not be afraid of money—but not the second. I had been a fool in virtually every way possible. If I could get money to do something related to religious diversity with youth involved, I got it. My MO was to get invited to high-profile conferences like the Clinton Global Initiative, sniff out the people giving away money, sidle up to them, and make a sizzling elevator pitch about Interfaith America.

In this way, we got resources from the Carnegie Corporation to do an Interfaith and Immigration project, from GMAC to do an Interfaith in the Rust Belt project, money from foundations interested in increasing the participation of American Muslims in civil society, grants from the State Department to run interfaith trainings in Europe and India, a partnership with the Tony Blair Faith Foundation to launch the Faiths Act Fellowships in Africa, and a set of campus programs, including the aforementioned Interfaith Campus Fellowship.

Because the dollars came quickly, and were temporary, we had to hire on the fly. The people who wound up staffing these projects had way more loyalty to their specific initiative than to the broader mission of Interfaith America. That may have been because Interfaith America, as an organization, didn't really have a mission. There really wasn't an Interfaith America, there were a dozen separate project teams that shared an office space. My job was to keep getting the grants and feeding a beast that kept growing and growing, and that I felt I had little control over, even though my title was founder and president.

Partially this is because I simply was not an effective institutional leader, and partially it's because this is how the world of philanthropy is set up. You get short-term money to run short-term initiatives. The money rarely even covers the full cost of the initiative—forget the additional dollars required to rent an office, hire an operations team, and pay the executive director.

The other problem was the frame. Fast money only comes when you are operating in someone else's frame. In the post–9/11 era, when Interfaith America first launched, the dominant frame was Islam and the West. Funders were looking for projects that fit that category. I was successful at quick fundraising because I was willing to articulate the work of Interfaith America within a frame that I was frankly deeply ambivalent about.

Jenn and David were doing things the opposite way. "We want you to tell us what you need to make the change you're after. Share with us your overarching strategy and what you will need to get there. Be sure to identify clear and measurable metrics so that we know what's working and what's not. We won't impose metrics upon you that you don't agree with."

"Oh yes," Jenn continued. "Tell us what you think it's going to cost. And don't be shy; we're not afraid of money. Build the plan for what you think it's going to take. For the organizations we ultimately invest in, we typically make three-to-five-year unrestricted gifts of up to approximately one-third of the total budget. Use that as a foundation to raise the rest."

I almost fell out of my seat. Interfaith America had literally just gone through a rigorous pro bono evaluation process with a McKinsey and Company team led by an Interfaith America board member, Tarek Elmasry. (I wrote about this in a previous book, *Sacred Ground*.) We had basically figured out that the course we were on as an organization—an office space for a random set of partially funded, barely affiliated initiatives—was unwise and unsustainable. There was no big vision, no overarching strategy, no signature programs, no pattern of activities. Almost a decade after Ron Kinnamon had asked me, "How is the world different when you are successful?" I was no closer to an answer.

The opportunity that Jenn, David, and the Einhorn Collaborative offered us dovetailed with another remarkable moment for Interfaith America. In January of 2009, I got a phone call saying that I had been appointed by President Obama to be on his Inaugural Faith Council. Obama had spoken eloquently about positively engaging America's religious diversity in his inaugural address. My appointment to the Faith Council was one part of the concrete follow-up to the vision he laid out about America embracing its religious diversity.

Interfaith cooperation now had a champion who sat in the Oval Office, and Interfaith America was his chosen vehicle for implementation. And we had a funder who had offered to put a significant amount of gas in the tank.

Interfaith America developed a strategic plan that would have us concentrate our network of programs in the world of higher education. We spoke of college campuses as laboratories of interfaith cooperation and launching pads for interfaith leaders. We laid out a plan that worked within the grooves of the sector: we would consult with campus administrations on interfaith strategic plans, engage student affairs staff and students on interfaith leadership trainings, and partner with higher ed associations on making sure that religion was a part of the diversity conversation.

We made a call to the State Department to return part of the grant they had given us for the India Interfaith Training Initiative ("I don't think this has ever happened before," a surprised government official told us). We politely cut ties with the Tony Blair Faith Foundation. We told GMAC that we no longer did community-based programs and the Carnegie Corporation that we were not an issue-focused organization. It is no fun to unwind programs. It is literally unheard of to return money. I relished none of this. But when a funder gives you $10 million over five years and says, "Come back and show me how the world is different when you implement your vision through your proposed programmatic strategy," you know you have the chance of a lifetime.

Initially, I thought that executing a strategic plan would feel restricting. The truth is that I found it liberating. As Ron Kinnamon would often tell me, a strategic plan is not just about what we do, it's about what we *don't* do. That meant that I didn't have to agonize over every speaking invitation; equipped with a plan that prioritized higher education, I knew that my job was to speak principally on campuses and at higher ed conferences. Having settled that question, we could problem-solve on what to do with invitations from congregations and high schools. It turns out that our growing alumni network was looking for speaking opportunities and that many houses of worship and AP history teachers were very happy to have a recent college grad talk about the story of their interfaith leadership. And so the Alumni Speakers Bureau was born.

A strategic plan also requires you to develop genuine expertise in your stated area of focus. When Interfaith America was running a dozen different projects, we were basically doing Interfaith 101 across the board. Nothing had much intellectual depth or long-term strategy. Having chosen to focus on higher education and having decided to follow the general pattern of other civic institutions in terms of signature programs and special initiatives, the areas we were lacking in became abundantly clear. We had robust signature programs for campus administrators, student affairs staff, and students. We had built out our alumni network through initiatives like the speaker's bureau. But we were doing virtually nothing at the faculty level, and we were painfully short on contributions to scholarship.

One of our board members, Donna Carroll, president of Dominican University, gently brought this up at a board meeting. The people who define a university are the faculty, she said. If Interfaith America doesn't have signature programs that work with faculty, it's hard to be taken seriously in the world of higher education.

It was propitious timing. In January of 2013, I gave a talk at Yale titled "Toward a Field of Interfaith Studies." It argued that the interactions between religiously diverse people in democracies were of increasing interest to scholars from disciplines ranging from anthropology to theology, but these scholars were rarely in conversation with one another. That was a problem that needed to be rectified, because such interactions would only increase and were bound to have a profound impact on everything from the identities of individuals to the durability of faith communities to the shape of civil society and the tenor of public life. I proposed an interdisciplinary field called interfaith studies that would gather scholars from a range of disciplines who shared the subject matter interest of religiously diverse people in interaction. Interfaith studies, I suggested, might look similar to educational studies or public health, fields where expert faculty launched research projects, taught classes, designed effective real-world interventions, and trained a cadre of professional practitioners.

The talk was published in the journal *Liberal Education* and started to generate buzz amongst academics interested in lived religion.[8] Sensing an opportunity, Interfaith America approached a major higher education association (the Council of Independent Colleges) and a funder (the Henry Luce Foundation) with a big idea: let's create a faculty seminar that would help academics interested in research and teaching about religious diversity develop courses in the emerging field of interfaith studies. In addition to CIC, a whole set of scholars who had written about religion—Diana Eck, Catherine Cornille, and Laurie Patton—agreed to partner with us.

The first year, we had more than twice as many applications as we could accept. And the numbers have only grown from there. The Luce Foundation renewed its grant, and when that renewal was up, the Lilly Endowment took over the funding, with the suggestion that they viewed this as a long-term endeavor.

What started as a two-year special initiative to fill an obvious gap in Interfaith America's programming—working with faculty—has become a signature program. There are now over three hundred faculty who have gone through the Teaching Interfaith seminar. There are at least that many interfaith studies courses being taught. Dozens of colleges have minors in interfaith studies. The *New York Times* did a profile on the first major in interfaith studies, at Elizabethtown College.[9] There is also a burgeoning world of scholarship, with journals, books, academic societies, and national conferences.

All in all, it is an excellent example of how an institution can help to build a field.

FIELD BUILDING

If you had asked me to draw you a picture of success when I first started Interfaith America in the late 1990s, I would have probably shown you something like the 1963 March on Washington with me at the podium. That's how I thought about social change as a young person. I loved being in the spotlight, pointing the way forward, thousands of cheering people following behind. I loved being thought of as a symbol of progress; I loved being called a prophetic voice.

I'm a lot more careful about all of that now. First of all, it takes a ton of energy to be a public symbol and I'm actually a pretty private person. It makes me nervous to be recognized in an airport. Second, I think there are probably very few genuinely prophetic voices in our world. I'm certainly not one of them. And most of those who regard themselves as prophetic voices, in my experience, are just people with big mouths and lots of opinions.

My friend Matt Weiner, now the associate dean for religious life at Princeton, was one of the first people I discussed Interfaith America with, all the way back in 1998. It was all about me at that time—my story, my mile-a-minute ideas, my speaking ability. When I visited him at Princeton twenty years later and laid out some of the big changes at the organization, he said to me: "You've completed the Weberian cycle within a single institution, and in your own person. You've gone from charismatic leader to institutional leader within twenty years." It was one of the highest compliments I've ever received.

I think about what Interfaith America does now as building the field of interfaith cooperation, and, in a broader sense, contributing to the wider field of bridge building in a diverse democracy. In 2004, David Bornstein published a book called *How to Change the World*, about an organization called Ashoka and its big idea: social entrepreneurship. The program that Ashoka sought to scale focused on seeking out and selecting exceptional social entrepreneurs as Ashoka Fellows. But the program itself would never grow big enough to change the world, no matter how many Ashoka Fellows get elected. To change the world, you needed a whole field of institutions dedicated to the idea of social entrepreneurship. The conclusion of Bornstein's book was about Ashoka's success as measured by the growth of the broader field of social entrepreneurship.[10]

By the early 2000s, several organizations (most notably, Echoing Green and the Skoll Foundation) had emerged that effectively copied Ashoka's approach of selecting and supporting exceptional social entrepreneurs. Elite bodies like the World Economic Forum launched social entrepreneurship arms too, and well-known foundations like Ford started referring to some of their grantees as social entrepreneurs. The term started being used regularly by government officials and major newspapers. The pattern change was obvious in the academy too. There were social entrepreneurship courses, conferences, and centers at colleges across the country. Professors like Greg Dees at Duke were putting social entrepreneurship at the heart of their research, and journals like the *Stanford Journal on Social Innovation* were emerging as well.

As Interfaith America's funding base expanded and stabilized, my eye has turned to field building. The goal has not been to put a million people in the street or for me to give the highest-profile speech imaginable; it has been to help institutionalize interfaith cooperation, first in the sector of higher education and then in adjacent spaces like religious communities, civil society organizations, public health, and for-profit companies.

We're working toward this goal in a number of different ways, many of them behind-the-scenes. We write letters for the files of faculty in our network who are going up for tenure, encouraging their deans and provosts to include the term "interfaith studies" in their title. We review manuscripts and connect scholars of interfaith studies to publishers, often blurbing the book when it is released. We consult with philanthropic entities, encouraging them not only to make grants to Interfaith America but also to establish stand-alone giving areas in interfaith work. In fact, one of Interfaith America's greatest accomplishments is working with the Arthur Vining Davis Foundations to rename their theology giving program, "Interfaith Leadership and Religious Literacy." When philanthropy identifies an area of work and gives it resources, it helps to build a field.

Amongst the most important things that we do to build the field of interfaith work is to give away huge numbers of mini-grants. We give away mini-grants to student groups that attend the Interfaith Leadership Initiative so they can return to their campuses and run interfaith service and dialogue programs; to Interfaith America alumni who have a creative interfaith idea for their faith community or city; to faculty members who are starting or strengthening an interfaith studies course; and to campus administrators who want to engage in an interfaith strategic planning process.

Grant making is more than a signature program at Interfaith America, it is an overarching strategy. We do it in virtually every one of our initiatives. It encourages new people to start programs, allows veterans to sustain their work, and encourages everyone involved to see interfaith leadership as a legitimate, professionalized field. For virtually every grant program, Interfaith America does some sort of gathering. This gives us an opportunity to expand and strengthen the network of people who view themselves as builders of the field of interfaith cooperation, to learn from their experience, and to distill those learnings into the programs we run and the books we write. The learnings also get baked into the next requests for proposals we design. In this way, we have a built-in feedback loop. We are always utilizing the learnings from the field to set new standards of excellence.

Finally, we are involved in original research in a significant way. Along with Professors Matthew Mayhew and Alyssa N. Rochenbach, we launched the Interfaith Diversity Experiences and Attitudes Longitudinal Study (IDEALS). Spanning five years and involving three administrations of students at over 120 campuses, it was the most comprehensive research project of religious diversity in higher education ever done. Graduate students and scholars will be using the data set for years to come. Amongst the key findings of the survey: nearly three-fourths of college students say they spend time focusing on racial diversity, but fewer than half report learning anything about religious diversity. It was a clarion call for higher education to invest more time in this area—in other words, an invitation to further build the field.[11]

TO WORK AS A TEAM, PLAY LIKE THE DEAD

When the leaders of different organizations gather together, a favorite activity is arguing about which metaphor best describes how your staff works together. Is it like a professional athletic team where the staff are different players competing, year after year, for starting spots and high salaries? Is it like the military where the generals call the shots and the soldiers go where they're told?

Interfaith America, I say, is none of the above. We work together the way the Grateful Dead play.

I saw the Dead for the first time at Soldier Field in the summer of 1992 and have been a devotee of both the music and the philosophy ever since.

Dead shows are absolutely unique. Most bands on tour play the same twenty songs night after night, switching maybe three or four out, max. This is true for even exceptional bands like U2.

The Dead never played the same show twice. Their entire song-book of several hundred tunes was available to them, and they basically played twenty different songs every night, rarely repeating the same one during the same week. And the Dead never played the same song the same way twice. They invented the live, extended rock and roll jam.

Think about how well you have to know your songs to be able to riff and jam on any given one at any given time. Think about how well you have to know your songbook to play twenty different tunes a night, night after night, for an entire summer. Think about how well you have to know your fellow musicians to pull any of this off.

I've long looked to Dead shows as a model for how I approach public speaking. I have a set of forty or fifty stories about interfaith cooperation in my head, and when I'm keynoting at a campus or a conference, I'll string six or seven different stories together into what I hope is a coherent whole. I do this in part because it's a way of proving to myself that I fully understand Interfaith America's vision, mission, and strategy. If I have to constantly find stories that illustrate our work, string several together into a speech that inspires other people, and do it night after night without too many repeats, well then, I feel comfortable with my own mastery of our work.

But the most important reason I do this is because each audience and its context are different. My goal is to get across the same basic

vision—America as an interfaith nation, defined by religious pluralism, built by civic interfaith leaders, with campuses serving as laboratories and launching pads—to audiences that range from presidents
of foundations to first-year college students. I think of the stories I
string together as a concert setlist that communicates an interfaith
vision meant to inspire that particular audience.

But I'm not a solo act. What made the Dead special is that they
were a band. They *all* had to know every song, they *all* had to be able
to jam, and they had to have the combination of individual virtuosity and group chemistry to be able to do it together. That's how
well the leadership team of a nonprofit organization should know its
songbook—its mission and strategy, its core concepts and theories, its
signature programs and pattern of activities.

One of the great myths of a nonprofit is that the mission gives the
staff a natural focus, much the way the profit motive naturally focuses
a lot of companies. The truth is much messier. That's because any
mission has a hundred interpretations, and any strategy can lead to a
thousand possible jams.

The Dead had hundreds of songs and thousands of jams, and yet,
they always sounded like the Dead.

As Ron Kinnamon explained to me with respect to the Y, a nonprofit *has* to reinterpret its mission and strategy as times change, but
through it all it has to know and retain its identity.

At Interfaith America, we believe that religious diversity is a fundamental American strength. We partner with key institutions, starting with higher education, to ensure America lives up to its interfaith
potential.

The first task of people who are part of an organization with a
mission is to learn the songbook. *This is not easy, but it is an absolute
requirement.*

If you want to play different music, then you should go join a different band. In the Interfaith America context, if you want to do
diversity work that cancels people rather than builds relationships,
then you should work somewhere else. That doesn't make you a bad
person, and it doesn't make us a bad organization. We know the music

we want to play. It's country blues. I like heavy metal too, but that's not what we play here. If that's what you want to play, there are plenty of great bands out there for you to join.

The second task is to get good at playing your instrument. If you are part of the program team at Interfaith America, getting good at playing your instrument means learning how to teach interfaith case studies, give interfaith keynotes, facilitate interfaith dialogues, gather people who run interfaith projects, and discern the best practices and learnings from those convenings. If you are part of the leadership team at Interfaith America, add management, strategy, budgets, external partnerships, and funding to the set of things you need to excel at.

You can take this "learn the songbook and play your instrument well" analogy one step further—to the roots. The Grateful Dead studied and played country, blues, rock, jazz, and bluegrass. These are the roots of the music, the literatures and traditions that shaped the Dead's music.

Interfaith America comes out of a variety of literatures as well. So-cial capital theory. The branch of political philosophy that asks how you build a healthy diverse democracy. The parts of social psychology that explore how to build spaces that encourage different identity groups to cooperate. To really understand our songbook—our vision, mission, and strategy, as it manifests in key concepts, signature pro-grams, special initiatives, and significant partnerships—you should acquire a fluency in these literatures.

Thus far, I've focused on the live Dead—how their concerts can serve as a metaphor for the leadership of an organization really un-derstanding its work. But I think there's a lot to be learned from how the Dead wrote songs too.

Here is how that typically went. Jerry Garcia would come up with the framework and feel for a new song and then play it for the rest of the band. Those members would then figure out their part in the song—Phil the bass line, Mickey and Bill the drums, Bobby the rhythm guitar. There was an initial essence and shape that gave focused guidance, but there was room for the other band members to create their own role. Again, think of the virtuosity this demanded of different band members and the chemistry that it required of the group as a whole.

In my mind, here's the crucial thing: everybody had to have a bone-deep sense of what constituted a Grateful Dead song. The part you are creating is not principally about what you feel like playing, but rather what you are adding so that the whole comes out to be something distinct to the Dead. The only reason that the "figure out your own part" approach worked is because everyone had such a deep sense of the defining qualities of a Grateful Dead tune.

One of the things that has struck me about many nonprofit organizations is that lots of staff think of themselves as solo acts. They run their initiatives the way they want to, relatively unconcerned with the whole. I understand this. Nonprofits attract people who care about the mission of the organization and have their own creative ideas about how that ought to be expressed in the world. And because hierarchy and internal order are generally far more fluid than at a for-profit company, many nonprofits turn out to be a physical space that holds together a set of solo acts running disconnected initiatives. That's like a band being a set of musicians each playing what they feel like playing, unconcerned about the broader whole of the song.

The Grateful Dead were a set of exceptional musicians who had a great deal of latitude to carve out their own part for any particular song. It worked because of their respect for one another's virtuosity and because of their total commitment to the song.

This leads to the next point. Everyone plays a crucial role in the operation, but not everyone writes songs or plays on stage in front of tens of thousands of people. Some people organize the tour, some people set up the stage, some are backing musicians on certain songs. These are all important roles, but they take their lead from the band.

Part of what made the Dead special is that not only did they change how concerts were done; they also changed the whole way a band approached its fans and the world. They were one of the first bands to start a mailing list and sell tickets directly to fans. They allowed people to tape their shows. They famously had a world-class speaker system called "the wall of sound."

Certainly, the band members didn't come up with all of these ideas; other people in the broader Dead operation did. But those people took their lead from the band. If someone in the broader operation had said, "Hey, we should do a laser show at our concerts," someone in the band would have probably said, "Look, we're not Pink Floyd; we're the Grateful Dead."

I think this metaphor helps us solve one of the principal challenges of any organization—how to help new members become thriving parts of the operation. Here are the rules for success: learn the songbook, become excellent at playing *this* music, take your lead from the band, be curious about the literatures that we come out of, get a bone-deep feel for what "our song" is, learn how to create your own part so that it contributes to the whole.

People who don't work out don't learn the songbook and show no curiosity about where it comes from; they want to play different music or simply can't get proficient at the music we play; they want to lead their own band or be a solo act; or they just don't want to take their lead from the people in this band.

The Dead created a new genre of American music and a new way of being a band. There are a thousand bands that were influenced by the way the Grateful Dead worked together—a thousand bands, and at least one civic institution.

CHAPTER THREE

JEN BAILEY, CRITIC AND BUILDER

IT WAS A DEEPLY MOVING LETTER.
  Jen Bailey was leaving the Interfaith America staff. She had been one of our first program participants, a member of the Chicago Youth Council (CYC), back in 2003 when the organization worked with high school students. Those were the days when I did everything from pick kids up from their homes to purchase snacks for our meetings.

That program, Jen wrote, had breathed life into her at a time when she had been gasping for air. Too often, she had felt awkward and out of place as a young Black woman in her high school. Her beloved grandfather passed away during those years. It was a time of intense distress. The sacred space and intense relationships of the CYC were a lifeline.

Jen joined the Interfaith America staff after graduating from college because she wanted to give to young people what Interfaith America had given to her. She arrived right at the moment when we were sunsetting our intensive leadership programs. Important as programs like the CYC were to the small group of participants involved, from the vantage point of our new strategic plan, they looked like simply one more hard-to-categorize item in the random collection of disparate initiatives Interfaith America was housing.

This felt like sacrilege to Jen. In her farewell letter to me, she wrote powerfully about the young people who lived, as she had, on the edge of a cliff of despair and needed an intentional sacred space and the opportunity to be deeply known by a caring mentor that the

CYC provided. That was what interfaith work was about to her, and Interfaith America was, in her words, "forfeiting the opportunity" to truly embrace it.

It was powerful for me to listen to the experience and hear the vision at the heart of Jen's critique, because critique was mostly what I got from Jen during her year on the Interfaith America staff. Jen was part of a group of recently hired employees who made it clear that they did not like the transition Interfaith America was making, the one I wrote about with obvious pride in the previous chapter.

It was a profoundly challenging time at the organization. To the outside world, we were a soaring success. Interfaith America had a seat at the table in the White House. McKinsey and Company had done their pro bono evaluation and given us a path to large-scale impact. Jenn Hoos Rothberg and the Einhorn Collaborative were offering to give us the funding to make that happen. Interfaith America had its first proper management team and had done the painstaking work of aligning our operations, our programs, and our long-term vision.

And it was an especially heady time for me personally. I was profiled by the *New York Times*, named one of America's best leaders by *U.S. News & World Report*, on the cover of *Sojourners Magazine* and the *Christian Century*, awarded the Louisville Grawemeyer Prize in Religion for my book *Acts of Faith*, named to President Obama's Inaugural Faith Council, and invited to the first state dinner with Indian prime minister Manmohan Singh. My speaker's fee had tripled, and so had my speaking invitations. All of this was taking place during sleepless, joyful, exhausting nights, as my wife, Shehnaz, and I had our second child in the spring of 2010.

The warmer the applause from the outside world, the colder the shoulder from my own staff. I think that's why I found Jen's letter so meaningful. It gave me the opportunity to discern the positive vision at the heart of her sometimes raw critique. Before Jen formally left staff and headed off to Vanderbilt Divinity School, I took her to lunch and offered the same advice that Yoland Trevino had given me fifteen years earlier: I told her that her vision was powerful, and that she should build it. Doing the work of intensive discussions about identity and spiritual wholeness with small groups of young people was not the work of Interfaith America anymore, but it should be someone's work—why not hers?

And build it she did. In 2016, Jen launched Faith Matters Network (FMN) with the purpose of integrating wellness, spiritual wholeness, and intense relationship building across difference.

A few years later, I called her up and told her we needed the services of her organization. It was the summer of 2020, and the United States was in the middle of both a pandemic and a long-overdue racial reckoning. The moment unleashed an intense set of emotions within Interfaith America's staff and alumni network. People needed curated space for deep discussion, to feel known, to have their whole selves and their spirits tended to. At Interfaith America we had become expert at serving as strategic consultants to campus administrations on expanding interfaith programs. We had just launched our major research initiative, IDEALS, and the Interfaith Leadership Institute, the Teaching Interfaith faculty workshop, and our other signature programs were growing impressively. But we lacked expertise in what was most needed at the moment: intimate space for discussion about identity and wholeness, with particular attention to race. It was the reason that Jen had left the organization a decade earlier.

I marveled at the process Jen's organization had developed for people to have difficult conversations on sensitive subjects. I was awed at the way she and her staff created sacred space, even over Zoom, and asked profound questions in a precise way that helped people connect more deeply. It was the most time that we'd spent together since her year on staff in 2010. I wanted the full story of how Jen had gone from critic of what Interfaith America lacked to builder of something that the whole nation needed.

Jen took me all the way back to her elementary school days, in a small town called Quincy, located on the western edge of Illinois. She'd been one of the only Black girls in her school and had known racism in deep and ugly ways. She moved to Chicago as a teenager and attended an elite public magnet high school called Whitney Young, known widely as the school where Michelle Obama graduated. For college, Jen went to Tufts, which she describes as an alien world. It was a campus dominated by suburban white kids, and so many, according to Jen, carried a peculiar twist of entitlement and bitterness—entitlement because they felt that the world belonged to them, bitterness because they had wound up at Tufts rather than Yale or Harvard.

Black students like Jen were told often in no uncertain terms that they were only there because of affirmative action, even though many of them had *actually* been admitted to Harvard and Yale and had chosen to attend Tufts. It was a shocking feeling of marginalization. And it was from that feeling that Jen started coursework in critical theory, engaging with concepts like white supremacy, structural racism, and colonialism. It was a new lens not only on her experience at Tufts but also, in some ways, her whole life. She describes it as being "given the intellectual language to understand and name my own pain. A pain that, until then, had felt private, or secret."

She recalled the story of being removed from the gifted program at her middle school in Quincy—where she'd been one of the few Black kids to begin with—because one year her test scores dropped. The sense she got from her teachers was that the truth had finally come out, and that she hadn't belonged in gifted classes anyway. It wasn't until her mother marched into the principal's office with her entire history of testing that Jen got reinstated in those classes. The critical theory she was learning helped her frame her own experience and ask bigger questions: what about the Black kids who didn't have a mom like hers? Or whose teachers had made them feel so uncomfortable that it had affected their academic performance, their self-esteem, their whole life trajectory?

Here's how Jen characterized it: "There was something that was deep and real and powerful in my life that had for so long gone unnamed. It was how race and gender colored everything. Critical theory named those things and helped you realize that they were not just in your head. Critical theory says that it's the institution that's crazy—crazy with white supremacy, crazy with its history of discrimination. Critical theory gives you writers, thinkers, philosophers. It gives language and permission to question the status quo. I found it liberating, intellectually rigorous, unflinchingly honest about history, and profoundly personal in that it gave me the tools to name my own hidden, secret, shameful pain and place the blame on the rightful perpetrator—institutional racism and sexism."

It was directly from this experience that Jen came to Interfaith America. She was processing her life and the world through the lens of critical theory, and Interfaith America was going through a transition from multi-project scrappy start-up to an established national civic institution driven by a top-down strategic plan. It was an epic case of bad timing. Jen made the right decision to leave—and the right choice to go to Vanderbilt Divinity School, led by the Black womanist scholar Dean Emilie Townes.

It was at Vanderbilt that Jen started to see the limits of critical theory. She told me the story of being in an ethics class with a heavy focus on theory during her second year. One day that semester, the news report of a young girl being shot and killed on the South Side of Chicago hit Jen particularly hard. That afternoon, after her ethics class, Jen was meant to meet up with Aaron, a client of a hunger-related nonprofit she was working for at the time. Aaron wasn't able to feed his family and Jen was doing a food delivery. She sat in her ethics class, listening to a lecture on critical theory, and suddenly found herself thinking: "How is any of this useful to that girl on the South Side of Chicago, or to Aaron and his family?"

She was coming to the conclusion that critical theory was a helpful tool for analysis, but not construction. And she was coming up against the limits of each of her various worlds. The direct service organization she was working for might get Aaron and his family food for the night or the week, but it was not going to make a dent in food insecurity nationwide, or even just in Nashville. The critical theory courses she was taking focused so much on systems of oppression that they failed to see Aaron's full humanity, including his immediate needs. It was theory made for the classroom, not the world. And the church, as powerful as it was for Jen, was not an institution she wanted to lead. She wanted to be a scholar, but not in the classroom. A preacher, but not in a pulpit. She wanted to make a concrete difference in people's lives, but not be limited by the narrow focus of a direct services organization.

So she started to dream outside of those boxes. She had started meeting other young progressive faith leaders who possessed similar sensibilities. As she listened to their individual stories, she started to discern a broader narrative. She wondered whether some kind of organization that connected these diverse young faith leaders was her contribution to the world. Jen was taking steps down the path of what she would come to call "constructive theology."

As she was finishing at Vanderbilt, Jen applied for four different opportunities. Only one came through—a fellowship at the Nathan Cummings Foundation in New York. During that fellowship year, she talked to over fifty faith-based organizational leaders from across the nation and quickly discovered that she didn't want to build another faith-based community organizing outfit, or another faith-based advocacy institution. What she realized was missing from the landscape was the thing that she had gotten from the Chicago Youth Council and that Interfaith America had not continued on with: an institution that integrated relationship building across diversity with spirit-based wellness work and that had the capacity to tell a broader story to the world. She found a co-conspirator named Micky ScottBey Jones, and together they started building the Faith Matters Network.

"So much happened between the idea and the reality," Jen told me. She got engaged, moved to Nashville. Her mom fell sick, and later passed. Through all of this, she and Micky hustled. They turned speaking engagements into consulting gigs and put the money into the organization. They got activist residencies and used them to experiment with new program ideas. Jen jokes that the fancy term for this process is "iterative design" but that she and Micky always called it by its real name: "making shit up."

Jen's story of building the Faith Matters Network has a lot of parallels to the experience of building Interfaith America. Like us, FMN took a while to find its signature programs and along the way expended energy on matters that distracted from their main work. One of those included experimenting with a flat organizational structure. "I was stupid, okay," Jen told me, laughing. She continued: "One of my best friends, a Black woman who went to Stanford Business School, looked at me in horror when I told her that we had launched a for-profit arm to Faith Matters Network and were giving everybody on the team equity."

The problem, Jen learned, was not that flat organizational structures or equity arrangements were wrong or bad. It's that they took energy, and at the end of the day she decided that the limited energy of Faith Matters Network should be spent on its programs, initiatives like the People's Supper, which were taking off nationally and required an enormous amount of staff time and a clear hierarchy of decision-making power.

It was a clear hierarchy with Jen at the top. She was the person building the national partnerships, doing the major media interviews, bringing in the money. When she realized that the buck stopped with her, she embraced the responsibility (she quoted the line from *Spiderman* to me, "With great power comes great responsibility") and made some deliberate decisions about the kind of leader she wanted to be.

"It was a womanist approach, with a pastoral sensibility," she told me. "I know that I'm ultimately in charge, but I want to bring a variety of voices into leadership decisions. I want my way of leading to help us live our core values of accompaniment, spiritual sustainability, and connection."

Jen and I were talking a month before the date she was due to give birth to her first child. The way she made decisions about the structure of FMN during her maternity leave illustrates her leadership style. The way most nonprofits would have handled the matter was to appoint or hire an interim executive director, someone who was clearly in charge. But Jen wanted to explore a range of options. She brought her team together and asked the question: How do we use my maternity leave as an opportunity to help you lean into your own leadership? What they discerned was that each one of them was excited about their own opportunities for further development and were eager for coaching to help them down that path. So instead of appointing a single interim director, they decided to invite in an experienced mentor/elder. "This is not a role that's in the nonprofit leadership handbook," Jen joked with me, "but it's the right decision for this organization and this team at this point in our development."

This is all part of what Jen refers to as her tool kit of Black womanist constructive theology. The tools, Jen emphasizes, come from centuries-old traditions that are simply not typically thought of as methods for organizational effectiveness, and yet they have sustained oppressed people across generations. Jen cites as an example something she calls "mother wisdom," a phrase that she borrowed from Alice Waters. It's an approach grounded in the lived experience of Black women in the United States. It's the belief that you can make a way out of no way. It includes the plainspoken lines of wisdom Jen's grandmother would share with her. Lines like "Go sit your butt down," when it was clear that Jen was getting too wound up about something, a test or a job interview. "Sit your butt down," Jen told me, is mother wisdom for "It's time for self-care."

Mother wisdom is deeply woven into the practice of religious communities and the narratives of religious traditions. Mother wisdom is there in Hagar arguing with God in the desert, her child faint with thirst. Mother wisdom is there in the presence of the women who took care of the body of Jesus after the crucifixion. It is no accident to Jen that it was women who first discovered him risen.

Mother wisdom is there in the miracle of loaves and fishes, a miracle that Jen saw performed on a weekly basis as Black church mothers turned two boxes of spaghetti and a loaf of bread into a dinner feast for hundreds.[1]

And mother wisdom is present in my favorite initiative that Jen Bailey launched at Faith Matters Network—the People's Supper. Amidst the outright rage that erupted amongst progressives after Donald Trump was elected, Jen had the presence of mind to step back and recognize that, as she later told Krista Tippett of *On Being*, the question of the twenty-first century was "How can we be together?"[2] You cannot build a better order out of a constant, vicious cycle of racism and resistance. Spaces needed to be created for people to connect in new ways. Mother wisdom recognizes that everybody needs to eat and everybody has a story. From these elemental truths, beautiful things can be created.

Jen and the Faith Matters Network staff teamed up with veteran community builder Lennon Flowers, founder of the Dinner Party, and created the People's Supper. The purpose was to, in the words of the Irish poet Pádraig Ó Tuama, find a way "of navigating our differences that deepen our curiosity, deepen our friendships, deepen our capacity to disagree, deepen the argument of being alive."[3]

Often, a People's Supper will have facilitators who guide the gathering through a series of questions and prompts. "Who are your people?" the facilitator might ask. Or, "Describe a time when you have felt excluded, and tell us about a moment when you have felt radically welcome." The facilitators also set ground rules: We should not expect perfection from ourselves, others, or even the space where we come together. We should not claim innocence or speak only of our scars. We should recognize that truth and love are things that can be increased when we connect in the right ways. Our highest hope should be to grow together. In other words, to create a civic space where we can be a community. Depending on who constitutes the gathering, a People's Supper might have opening and closing rituals, perhaps even an altar where people are invited to place objects that are meaningful to them.

I think the signature genius of the People's Supper is that virtually anyone can host one and adapt it to their particular purposes or needs. Elite companies have hosted People's Suppers to break down the toxic internal competition endemic to such cultures. Interfaith groups have hosted them to talk through doctrinal and political divides. People who have experienced violent trauma have developed a set of specific questions to guide their own gatherings. The mayor of Erie, Pennsylvania, named among the most racially tense cities in the nation, asked Faith Matters Network to hold a series of suppers to bridge racial divides. The town of Creede, Colorado, population four hundred, has experienced the ideological divide at the level of daily personal interaction in a manner that could literally tear the place apart. The residents have organized a series of People's Suppers to build their sense of community back up again. A People's Supper was a cornerstone of the work that Jen did with Interfaith America in the summer of 2020.

"What's your mother wisdom on critique?" I asked Jen. She responded that she sees it as an important tool because it helps us analyze the spiritual and material conditions we live in, but it has profound limits. It too often divides rather than includes, and deconstructs rather than builds. When she encounters people who lead with critique, the first thing Jen does is wonder whether they are simply playing the disrupter role in a healthy ecosystem of social change. If they want the role of critique to be the entire ecosystem, or the entire tool kit, Jen says she gives it the side-eye. She doesn't have time for it. It's not what Faith Matters Network is about. They are looking to put their energy into building a world, not tearing one down. Jen puts it this way: "Yes, the world is messed up, but as people of faith, when we say collective liberation we really mean *collective*, we really mean everybody." She quoted the mantra of the Black feminist writer Toni Cade Bambara: our job is to make the movement irresistible to everyone.[4]

CHAPTER FOUR

CAMPUS AS CRUCIBLE

I HEARD ABOUT THE PROTEST A DAY BEFORE ARRIVING ON campus. A group called the Diaspora Coalition at Sarah Lawrence College, an elite liberal arts school about an hour's drive north of Manhattan, had put out a list of demands online and announced that they were going to occupy a campus building.[1]

I had been invited to campus by President Cristle Collins Judd to be part of a series called "Differences in Dialogue." My interlocutors were Washington University political philosopher and law professor John Inazu and Nancy Cantor, the president of Rutgers University–Newark and also an alumna of Sarah Lawrence. Both are friends and colleagues. John is probably a click or two more conservative than I am, and Nancy maybe a click or two more liberal, but we all view the racism and conspiracy theories of the current Republican Party as anathema.

I've been to many campuses where protests had made national news (Yale, Princeton, Swarthmore, Oberlin, Amherst, maybe a dozen or so more), but I have never actually been in the middle of one myself, at least not since my own undergraduate days at the University of Illinois. So I approached with a sense of curiosity.

The event was well attended. There were Sarah Lawrence board members, people from the local community, students, and faculty all streaming into the auditorium. A handful of friendly student activists were outside the doors handing out copies of the Diaspora Coalition's manifesto. I saw many more heading up the stairs to fill the balcony area of the theater. It all felt very neighborly.

The most powerful story told during the panel discussion was by John Inazu about his father, who had died only a few weeks earlier after a long battle with cancer. He had been born in Manzanar, one of the ten camps where Japanese Americans were forcibly interned during World War II. His parents were prevented from holding him as a baby. John shared this detail in a steady, even voice, a tone that sharpened the tragedy and injustice of the situation.

Somehow John's father went on to become the kind of American patriot who joins the military and remains committed to it for the rest of his life. John's brother is a cop. John himself is military and even worked for a time at the Pentagon. But in divinity school at Duke University, he came under the influence of Stanley Hauerwas, who asked how a Christian like John could reconcile his faith, which ought to commit him to pacifism, with what was, for Hauerwas, an idolatrous involvement with the American military. It was a lot for John to consider. When John tried to talk about it with his father, it became clear that it was not a conversation his father was interested in having. For him—this man who had been born in a Japanese internment camp and not held as a baby because of a racist policy of his government—questioning the American military in any form was borderline treason.

The story shook me to my core, highlighting just how complex people are and how unwise it is to pretend to guess at people's views based on their identities or experiences. "I was born in the Manzanar internment camp and that's why I am a supporter of the American military to my bones" is a statement that sounds so jarring to everything I think I know about identities and politics.

I had hoped that we could unpack issues like this one with the audience during the question-and-answer period. But there was a rustle in the balcony and a discernible shift in mood right as that part of the program began. Before an audience member could ask a question, sixty students stood up as a collective, launched their fists in the air, and declared that they were taking over the space. They began reading, one by one, statements of protest from their smartphones. Each statement followed the same formula. A typical one went like this: "As a person who benefits from white privilege but is oppressed by heteronormativity, I call out Sarah Lawrence College for further oppressing its already marginalized students and call on President Cristle Collins Judd and the college to immediately agree to all demands issued in our manifesto."

Eight students read statements, many of which began with a ritual confession of white privilege (a pattern that served mostly to underscore the fact that most of the speakers were white). After each statement there were choreographed "No justice, no peace" chants, punctuated by the waving of fists in the air.

About half the students directed insults at President Judd, whom some called with a sneer "Cristle." When President Judd stood and said in a sharply contrasting tone of earnest politeness something to the effect of, "We hear you. Thank you for making your views known. I have met with you before and will meet with you again to discuss your demands. Now can we allow members of the audience who have questions of our panel to ask them?" she was met with a set of louder jeers.

The night closed with a spokesperson of the Diaspora Coalition demanding of the panelists on stage that we go on record, immediately and publicly, in support of their manifesto. A dozen cell phones were up, recording the moment. John, Nancy, and I somehow managed to communicate that we appreciated the students' energy and resolve but hadn't studied the manifesto enough to sign on.

The next morning, my Interfaith America colleague Noah Silverman and I were scheduled to meet with a smaller group of faculty, administrators, and students. The driver who picked us up from the hotel to take us to the meeting joked with us, "Did you know the students are asking for free detergent? Why can't they be like the rest of us and just hand-wash their clothes with regular soap when they run out?

"But what do I know," she continued. "I'm just an hourly employee with a high school education. These Sarah Lawrence kids are going to run the world. In fact, they already do." I couldn't tell if it was bitterness or irony in her voice. I'm pretty sure it wasn't pride.

It occurred to me that the Sarah Lawrence students had quite naturally assumed the position of the weaker party vis-à-vis more powerful academic administrators. But by going public in a self-righteous way, the students had widened their audience to individuals who had a very different understanding of what constituted identity privilege and who held it.

To the high school–educated hourly employee who drove around Sarah Lawrence students and visitors, it was the people they were driving, regardless of race, gender, or sexuality, who had the power.

I had a sudden realization about the protest the night before. Of all the important social identities and related dynamics that were named (heteronormativity, cis-genderism, white privilege), not a single one of the many students who spoke mentioned attending Sarah Lawrence as an identity and the role that particular identity would play in their lives.

That role is likely to be very significant.

In his book *Our Kids*, Robert Putnam observes that the American socioeconomic order can be neatly sorted into three categories. Those who have a high school education or less occupy the lower third; those with some college the middle third; and those who have completed college the upper third. A host of other quality-of-life indicators—occupation, income, health, social status, self-identity—are quite straightforwardly predicted by level of education.[2]

These findings include people with *any* kind of college degree. If you are at a name-brand selective institution, your chances of success in the knowledge economy are significantly higher than the individual who goes to a local commuter college. Consider this: there are just over 2,500 four-year residential nonprofit institutions of higher education in the United States, what most people reading this publication normally think of as college (I am not counting the several thousand for-profit institutions). If you attend a top-250 institution, you are in the top 10 percent; if you attend a top-25 institution, well, you are surely smart enough to do the math in your head. If the selectivity of these schools in any way maps onto success in the current economy, you have just positioned yourself in the upper reaches of the top third of American society.

If you are at an elite college like Sarah Lawrence, you probably know this, which is why you went to the trouble of positioning yourself to be admitted to such an institution in the first place.

Money is typically considered half of the social identity known as class; the other half is prestige. And this is where attending an elite college makes an unambiguous difference and is most certainly what our driver was chafing against.

In *The Tyranny of Merit*, the political philosopher Michael Sandel argues, "Elites have so valorized a college degree—both as an avenue for advancement and as the basis for social esteem—that they have difficulty understanding the hubris a meritocracy can generate."[3]

Sandel claims college degrees, especially from prestigious institutions, have been "weaponized." He supports this claim by reporting a study in which social psychologists surveyed college graduates across both the United States and Europe, asking them how they felt about a range of disenfranchised groups, including obese people, gay people, and ethnic and religious minorities. Across nations, college educated people ranked those who are poorly educated as the group they liked the least. Moreover, while people reported some embarrassment at their other prejudices, they were proud of the fact that they looked down upon the poorly educated. After all, if you graduated from college, you've merited your good life. If you haven't, you deserve your fate.

Sandel writes that "higher education has become a sorting machine that promises mobility on the basis of merit but entrenches privilege and promotes attitudes toward success corrosive of the commonality democracy requires." That is an academic description of a dynamic that was, for our driver, felt as an increasingly visceral anger. Imagine what it's like to be the high school–educated hourly employee driving around Sarah Lawrence students who are discussing their oppression in the back of your van, thinking what you would give to trade places with them.

There is an argument that goes that educational privilege is not at all like race, gender, and sexuality because it is an *earned* identity rather than an ascribed one. I have a fondness for this line of thinking because, having attended a flagship state school and an elite graduate school, it happens to bestow virtue on a dimension of my identity. Earning one's privilege sounds a lot nicer than having it randomly assigned.

But then I remember that just as race, gender, and sexuality are identities that are given meaning by their socially constructed contexts, so too is level of education. Consider this: If you live in a hunter economy, your position in the socioeconomic hierarchy is likely determined by how well you hunt. If you live in a warrior society, your status is associated with your ability to fight. We happen to have been born into a unique time and place in which reading, writing, analyzing, and computing are king. If the social hierarchy were based on other skills—and most societies over the course of human history have been—many of us would be middling at best, perhaps even utter failures.

If I had to guess, I'd say that was probably the case for most of the protestors from the night before as well. They, like me, were made for the knowledge economy. Looked at through this lens, it is remarkable that they were somehow able to use the analytical and communication skills that placed them at the top of the class ladder to tell the world that they were at the bottom.

By this point, the van ride was over, we were at the college, and my head was already spinning.

President Judd met us at the door and engaged us in conversation before the morning session began. I asked her if she'd been disturbed by the behavior of the students the night before. Not especially, she replied. Sarah Lawrence was an activist campus, and she was proud of that. The only thing that frustrated her was that some of the students had spurned her offer to take part in budget conversations. "I don't disagree with many of their demands," she said to me. "But meeting all of them would cost millions and millions of dollars. I want them to be part of the process of how a college raises and apportions its funds. That's a learning opportunity for them."

The most strident student activists didn't see it that way. They had said to President Judd that it was *their* responsibility to make demands and *her* responsibility to make budgets. That attitude was cause for concern. President Judd wanted Sarah Lawrence graduates going into the world not only with high ideals but also excellent organizational skills.

The morning meeting was characterized by the kind of conversation I associate with an excellent liberal arts seminar—searching and civil, an exchange of interesting views in pursuit of deeper understanding, not mutual condemnation. President Judd attended, as did several faculty members and a handful of the students who had protested the night before.

One of them was a Muslim international student from South Asia, a region, culture, and religion I know something about. She had been part of the protests but had not been one of the people to speak. I asked her if she felt represented by the Diaspora Coalition, both in substance and style. Somewhat, she said, but not fully. I wondered whether it was part of her cultural identity to sneeringly call educational leaders by their first names. "That would never happen where I come from, and I don't like when it happens now," she told me. And then, as if she understood exactly the point I was getting at, she said: "In the name of supporting minority identities, I have been part of things that violate my own minority identity, including rudeness to teachers and other educational leaders."

"Why do the smart and insightful students at Sarah Lawrence sign on to the Diaspora Coalition's manifesto if they don't feel properly represented by either its style or its substance, especially since it's a document whose entire purpose is to accurately represent minority identities?" I asked.

She responded: "The truth is, I've spent a lot of time on this campus in circles of students of color talking about oppression and marginalization. There are many people of color experiences on this campus, but you're only allowed to talk about the kind where your oppression should lead to revolution. I'm just wondering right now what it's all doing for me."

Then she said, "But I could never share that feeling more widely. People on this campus walk around scared that they are going to be 'Sarah Lawrenced' by their friends for saying something wrong, and that could be anything, from listening to an artist that's supposed to be canceled to not showing up to a protest that you should have attended."

"What's being Sarah Lawrenced?" I asked.

"It's when people ignore you without telling you why. They just treat you like you're invisible. One day you have a group of friends that you eat lunch with, and the next day you are alone."

I have visited something like 150 campuses over the last ten years and I can confidently report that most days at most colleges are good days. My experience at Sarah Lawrence was the exception, not the rule. It was also, however, not entirely out of left field. I have been a part of several classroom discussions where a handful of strident activists effectively silenced a variety of voices in the name of promoting diversity. More than one student of color has quietly observed to me that, in the name of promoting minority identities, they have had to suppress part of their own.

This should concern us. A college ought to be a place where the half-formed thoughts of individuals are shared with the group, precisely so they can be fully baked by a community of learners who are happy to assume the good will of their interlocutors in the common pursuit of greater truth. What else is a campus, long-time college president Jake Schrum once told me, but a community of considerate conversation?

In his wonderful book *College: What It Was, Is, and Should Be*, Andrew Delbanco, the Alexander Hamilton Professor of American Studies at Columbia University, remarks that on any list of America's great contributions to human civilization—jazz, baseball, the

Constitution—our system of over 2,500 four-year residential colleges and universities would rank near the top.[4]

We Americans ask a lot of our colleges. They define what makes an educated person and do their best to raise a generation of students up to that standard. They advance a knowledge base for the rest of our society, help set the civic priorities of the nation, and serve as mini civil societies.

They are models for diverse democracy. Our higher ed institutions, precisely because they highlight how particular identities can welcome diversity, are in a position to teach, and to help young people practice, the art of strengthening the particularity of identity while encouraging building bridges across groups. Consider this: over half of the private colleges in the United States were started by religious communities, and remarkably few restrict admission to their own group. This is an astonishing feature of American society. Institutions created to form people within one tradition now commonly serve as platforms that bring together and advance people from a range of traditions. We have found an avenue for the expression of religious identity in a way that doesn't create Balkanization but instead facilitates bridging social capital.

The Catholic philosopher Alasdair MacIntyre says that "a central purpose of higher education (is) to initiate students into conflict." A diverse democracy will inevitably have countless legitimate conflicts. Precisely for this reason, civic spaces that specialize in teaching people how to engage in such conflicts through language and politics rather than violence are essential, and people who learn these skills are well-positioned to become a society's leaders. MacIntyre goes so far as to say that "only from the university can the wider society learn how to conduct its own debates, practical or theoretical, in a rationally defensible way."[5]

It is precisely because the underlying structure of the institution is so strong and stable that it can hold together such a wide array of identities and such radically divergent views. It is no wonder that John Courtney Murray, the great Jesuit philosopher, viewed universities as a symbol of the kind of political community required to hold together the diverse groups and divergent views that made up a healthy pluralism. It was in the university, Murray argued, that creeds could be at war intelligibly.[6]

Colleges are a place of awakenings. As Tara Westover writes in *Educated*: "Everything I had worked for, all my years of study, had been to purchase for myself this one privilege: to see and experience more truths than those given to me by my father, and to use those truths to construct my own mind. I had come to believe that the ability to evaluate many ideas, many histories, many points of view, was at the heart of what it means to self-create."[7]

And they are places that build the foundations for awakenings to come. In his book *The Second Mountain*, David Brooks tells the story of being forced to read a book by Edmund Burke that he truly hated when he was an undergraduate at the University of Chicago. He was a Marxist revolutionary at the time, and Burke was arguing for being respectful of received wisdom and the importance of preserving traditions. It was only when Brooks confronted the monstrosity of Chicago's housing projects as a young journalist that he returned to that book by Burke, this time with a totally different mindset. The revolution in housing that the projects promised had turned into a nightmare of gang wars and drug abuse because the people advancing the revolution had neglected the long-received wisdom that people take care of the things they work to own.

Here is how Brooks reflects on his paradigm shift: "I felt more formed by my college education twenty-five years out than I did on the day I graduated. . . . I am so grateful for a university that had the gall to force me to read a book that at the time I truly hated. A school can transform a life."[8]

I wonder how those students at Sarah Lawrence will remember that Differences in Dialogue event. Perhaps the story of John Inazu's father, a man born in an internment camp who later became a fervent and unquestioning supporter of the United States military, will have stayed with them the way that the Edmund Burke book stayed with

David Brooks. Perhaps they will turn it over in their minds and think to themselves, "People are not like Russian nesting dolls—an outer doll of physical identity containing only predictable inner dolls of experiences, politics, aesthetics, and so on. Instead, people are endlessly complex and fascinating. You can never tell simply from someone's group identity how they will experience the world, or know from their experience what conclusions they will draw."

Perhaps, as in my case, those students will go on to build something and say that the first time that they thought about the importance of budgets was when the president of their alma mater invited them to the table to discuss how their values might be reflected in the key operating document of the institution. Perhaps they will speak of it fondly, forgetting entirely how they spurned the invitation when it was first offered.

SECTION TWO

THE GOOD SOCIETY

CHAPTER FIVE

AMERICA, THE PEOPLE'S POTLUCK

HERE IS WHAT DIVERSITY LOOKS LIKE IN THE CITY OF Mostar, located in Bosnia and Herzegovina. If you work for the Croat Catholic fire department, you don't respond to the burning buildings of Bosnian Muslims, even if you happen to be closer. And if you work for the Bosnian Muslim fire department, you let the flames engulf Croat Catholic homes. They have their own fire department.

If you are Catholic, you go to school from 7:30 a.m. to 1:30 p.m. If you are Muslim, you study in those same buildings starting at 2 p.m. Catholics go to a nightclub called Pink Panther; Muslims go to a nightclub called Art. There are two soccer teams, two garbage collection companies, two hospitals. The entire city is divided along ethno-religious groups.[1]

The way diversity is engaged in the town of Willmar, Minnesota, where half of the nearly twenty-one thousand residents are recent immigrants, is very different. The differences, first of all, aren't an occasion for division; they are an opportunity for everyone to be seen, celebrated, and enlarged. The best illustration of this is the big, beautiful world map in the front lobby of the high school with pins marking the national backgrounds of the student body. Over thirty nations are represented.

Willmar's diversity is recognized as the future business and civic talent of the city. Fifty local businesses donated $1,000 each to start an entrepreneurship program in the school system. The student participants develop and pitch businesses plans; the most promising ones get financial backing.

A leading insurance company, Blue Cross and Blue Shield of Minnesota, funded a Good Ideas program in which Willmar citizens hold dinners in their homes and houses of worship (with traditional meals provided by the hosts) to discuss ways to strengthen and improve the city. Sarah Senseman, the community integration director at BCBS Minnesota, noted, "The town of Willmar looks like what the rest of greater Minnesota is going to look like in the next ten years." BCBS was invested in the health of Willmar, and they recognized that nurturing a positive pluralism was vital for collective thriving.

It's important to note that it's not just the long-time white Christian residents doing the leading, or the adapting. Abdirahman Ahmed is the Somali Muslim executive director of the Community Integration Center. The center's programs focus on helping Somalis integrate into Willmar and to help people from Willmar learn about Somali culture. They have English classes for Somali adults and Somali classes for non-Somalis. And they have sessions for everybody where people are encouraged to ask blunt questions about the cultural patterns of other groups.[2]

THE SIGNIFICANCE OF THE CIVIC IN A DIVERSE DEMOCRACY

The United States is the most religiously diverse nation in human history, and it is on the brink of becoming majority-minority ethnically and racially. Will our future look more like Mostar or Willmar? In Mostar, a network of institutions and civic space create de facto segregation. In Willmar, the same institutions and civic spaces—schools, businesses, youth programs—nurture pluralism.

Diversity, as Harvard professor Diana Eck writes, is simply the fact of people with diverse identities living together in close quarters. Pluralism, on the other hand, is the proactive and positive engagement of difference.[3] Here is how I define civic pluralism: people from different identities coming together in shared spaces and institutions, engaging in shared activities that promote general well-being and are marked by cooperative relationships.

The institutions that nurture pluralism do not fall from the sky or rise from the ground. People build them. It was a civic leader, high school principal Paul Schmitz, who decided to put that big, beautiful map of the world in the lobby. It was civic leaders who started the Community Integration Center.

In the previous section, I wrote about the process of becoming a builder and offered lessons from the frontlines of institution building.

In this section I employ a somewhat wider lens and offer a vision of what it looks like to build a healthy diverse democracy. This chapter focuses on the importance of building a network of institutions into a strong social infrastructure. In the next chapter, I write in more detail about the power of narrative for a diverse democracy. And in the third chapter of this section, I focus on religion as an exemplar institution.

All of these chapters hold up civic pluralism as the highest ideal for a diverse democracy to nurture. Athletic leagues, parks, community theaters, volunteer programs, social services, educational institutions, hospitals, even barbershops and hair salons—these are what make up "the civic." A Walmart, a McDonald's, a Starbucks, run right, counts as well.

The civic either builds on a consensus or builds toward one, meaning that most people are in general agreement about the broad purpose of the institution. That's one of the reasons that civic spaces are so crucial in a diverse democracy—people with different identities and opposing views are willing to enter them and participate in their activities together. If the civic space is effective, it builds bridges between diverse people and a bridge to a better future. As Kwame Anthony Appiah says, "Democracy is not about majorities winning and minorities losing; it's supposed to be a system in which each of us take responsibility for our common welfare. . . . What makes us a people, ultimately, is our everyday commitment to governing a common life together."[4]

Effective civic leaders recognize that diversity is not just the differences you like. Civic institutions don't flatten identity or demand uniformity; rather, they highlight the power of what the participants have in common and create a space where disagreements can be discussed without violence.

Jeffrey Stout says that managing disagreement is the defining quality of a diverse democracy. He writes, "Democracy takes for granted that reasonable people will differ in their conceptions of piety, in their grounds for hope, in their ultimate concerns, and in their speculations about salvation. Yet it holds that people who differ on such matters can still exchange reasons with one another, and do both of these things without compromising their integrity."[5] Constitutional principles need to be upheld and the right government structures need to be in place for the above to be accomplished, but Stout emphasizes that diverse democracy happens as much in his neighborhood soccer league as in the Supreme Court.

John Courtney Murray defines a civilization as people living together and talking together. In his view, conversation *is* civilization. A pluralistic civilization is especially challenging to build because it requires the ability to have a conversation between people with very different identities and experiences. Murray writes, "By pluralism here I mean the coexistence within the one political community of groups who hold divergent and incompatible views . . . Pluralism therefore implies disagreement and dissension within the community. But it also implies a community within which there must be agreement and consensus."[6] There are many dimensions to this underlying community that must have the strength to hold together diverse groups and divergent views. There is the political dimension, which includes things like rule of law, balance of powers, and minority rights. There is the symbolic dimension, which includes things like shared myths and commonly held symbols. And there is the civic dimension, which the sociologist Eric Klinenberg emphasizes.

In his book *Palaces for the People*, Klinenberg asks the question: "What conditions in the places we inhabit make it more likely that people will develop strong or supportive relationships, and what conditions make it more likely that people will grow isolated and alone?"[7] The answer, he says, has everything to do with what he calls our *social infrastructure*, the civic spaces and institutions that facilitate healthy interaction. Social infrastructure plays a central but largely invisible role in connecting diverse people, protecting vulnerable communities, and healing alienated individuals. Sometimes it can make the difference between life and death. During the Chicago heat wave of 1995, Klinenberg showed that people who lived in neighborhoods with a strong social infrastructure survived; people who lived in neighborhoods without comparable associations, institutions, and networks too often did not.

America's social infrastructure includes everything from institutions like Harvard to the civic space of a local school bus. In all of these there are inspiring stories like those of Willmar, Minnesota, and cautionary tales like in the town of Worthington, also located in Minnesota, about a hundred miles away.

Worthington has also experienced high levels of immigration in recent years. Don Brink drives a school bus in Worthington, and he uses this seat of power to make his views about the new arrivals known. "I say 'good morning' to the kids who will respond to me. But this year there are a lot of strange kids I don't recognize."[8] The children he greets are the sons and daughters of the white farmers he knows. The children he ignores are the ones with darker skin and broken English.

A school bus is a civic space. It can be organized in a way that brings people with different identities together, or that drives them apart. As the leader of the civic space, Don Brink is creating an environment that is the antithesis of pluralism—he does not welcome some identities, he does not foster relationships between different groups, he does not advance a sense of the school bus as a common good that everyone has a right to and a stake in.

POTLUCK NATION

Tom Friedman, who wrote the *New York Times* piece about Willmar, calls the town a successful American melting pot. I don't think that's the right metaphor, and metaphors matter. As Walter Lippman said, "The way the world is imagined will determine at any given moment what men will do."[9]

Willmar is not thriving because its recently arrived Hondurans and Burmese are melting away their distinctive identities. It's thriving because they are bringing those identities to the community in ways that make a contribution to the whole. After all, as Friedman himself notes, the lunch spots with the best Yelp reviews in Willmar are the Somali Star and the Azteca Mexican Restaurant.

A better metaphor for the kind of pluralism we see in Willmar—and that we should want to build across the country—is a potluck supper, not a melting pot. (Mostar can probably best be described as a separate-pots model of diversity.)

I know a thing or two about potlucks. As I discussed in chapter 1, after college I moved to Chicago and took a job teaching in an alternative high school where urban minority youth came to get their GEDs. It was fulfilling but exhausting work, and I was lonely and longing for the kind of community that I had found at the University of Illinois. I had a couple of friends in the same general situation. I lived in a modest apartment that had a small front yard and plenty of street parking. And I knew how to cook exactly one dish—my mom's famous masala potatoes (made famous by her, not me).

In the dead of winter in early 1997, I told my handful of friends that I'd cook up a large batch, clean up the kitchen and living room, and put out whatever plates and silverware I had. I asked each of them to bring a dish and a friend.

From that one winter Tuesday night, the potluck grew and grew and grew. In the spring, we held a solemn ceremony commemorating the passing of the Beat poet Allen Ginsberg. By the summer, well over fifty people were regularly gathering, bringing not just food but guitars, drums, big ideas, and more plates and silverware. A handful of people started coming early to help me prepare the space, and a different crew volunteered to stay late for cleanup duty. It all happened quite naturally—people taking responsibility for their part in the upkeep of the whole.

Somewhere along the way someone said that we should create a 24/7 container for the spirit we shared at Tuesday night potlucks. And thus, the idea for the Stone Soup Cooperative (remember the name Stone Soup—I'll return to it soon) was born. In September, we took over the lease at Our Lady of Lourdes Convent on North Ashland Avenue in the Uptown neighborhood and moved in. The Tuesday evening potluck tradition continued on in that space for some twenty years. Literally thousands of diverse people have come through—artists, activists, writers, CEOs, priests—to socialize around food and share dreams for a better world.

It's this experience that got me thinking that a potluck supper is about the best symbol there is for a diverse democracy. Potlucks are civic spaces that both embody and celebrate pluralism. They rely on the contributions of a diverse community. If people don't bring an offering, the potluck doesn't exist. If everyone brings the same thing, the potluck is boring. And what a nightmare it would be if you brought your best dish to a potluck and you were met at the door with a giant machine that melted it into the same bland goo as everybody else's best dish. The *whole point* of a potluck is the diversity of dishes.

Potlucks respect diverse identities by enthusiastically welcoming the gifts of the people who gather. They facilitate relationships between people by creating a space for eating and socializing and surprise connections. And they cultivate in people the importance of not just the individual parts and the connections between them, but the health of the whole as well. Everybody benefits from a clean kitchen, enough dishes and silverware, and a safe and open place to eat and socialize. When it comes to a potluck, these are the structures of the common good. Everybody plays a role in their upkeep.

And while there is no one-to-one connection between people's ethnic, racial, and religious backgrounds and the dishes they bring, it's probably the case that a potluck with mostly South Asians is going to have a somewhat different spread than a potluck with mostly South Americans.

Ideally, you'd have both South Asians and South Americans—and people from North Africa, the Middle East, the West Indies, and all sorts of points beyond and in between, bringing all sorts of dishes, everything from recipes they learned from their grandmothers to things they just made up. Because actually, the point of a potluck is not *just* the different identities in one place, but the connections between them. The way things click. I mean, how great is it if you bring your *amazing* dip, a centuries-old recipe, and someone else has brought their *awesome* home-baked crusty bread?

Sometimes these things are prearranged, and sometimes they just happen. The best potlucks are like that—a little bit planned, a little bit haphazard.

A potluck is sensitive to identities, but in a pragmatic rather than an ideological way. As the demographics of the group change, the dishes on the table are likely to reflect those changes. Moreover, people have to be generally aware of what the gathering does and does not eat. If there are plenty of people coming who don't eat pork for religious reasons, probably you choose to bring a different dish. If there are people who don't eat dairy or gluten, you make sure to carefully label those items. Some of these dynamics might guide how the gathering at a potluck takes shape. Maybe the gluten-free folks find themselves hanging out with one another, at least at first, because they've gathered around the same dishes. Zones for identity communities to thrive are positive. But barriers between identity groups are not. At a good potluck, there is plenty of free flow that facilitates people from different identities meeting one another.

A potluck is the ultimate civic form. No mayor or general or governor commands people to a potluck. People do it themselves. In fact, the genius of a potluck is the perfect illustration of civil society in a democracy—it is an activity that turns what might otherwise have been a random collection of people into a community *because of what they do together.*

People tend to bring their best dishes to potlucks—the format encourages this. Also, you don't look for reasons to *exclude* people from a potluck, or to cancel the event. In fact, you hope that the nature of the activity actually helps you like people who you might otherwise dislike. Dorothy Day spoke about the Catholic Worker Movement as a space where it is easier to be good. The potluck is a space where it is easier for people to cooperate.

STONE SOUP LEADERSHIP

Potlucks build communities; communities sustain potlucks. It is a beautiful, virtuous circle. But everything starts with a leader. In the case of a potluck, the leader is the person or group who hosts. This doesn't take a genius or a superstar. In my case, it was just an individual lonely enough to risk trying something new.

Whoever you are, you can learn a lesson from the greatest potluck leader of all time—the central figure of the Stone Soup story.

Perhaps you remember the Stone Soup story from kindergarten or Sunday school. It's mostly known as a children's story, but like a lot of stories meant for kids that have been passed down generation to generation, it offers deep wisdom about building a vibrant civilization. Allow me to tell it with my own interfaith, multicultural, civil society–building twist.

The story takes place in a village. The inhabitants are isolated from one another, and starving. They close their blinds, and they lock their doors. I imagine a father telling his family that he doesn't like the family across the street because they speak English with an accent. The mother from across the street tells her kids that she doesn't like the family around the corner because they call God a name she doesn't recognize.

Into this village comes a traveler, a woman with a pack on her back. She strolls into the town square, builds a fire, and carefully takes out the items she is carrying. A stone, a ladle, a cauldron. She takes the cauldron to the river and fills it with water, returns, and places the cauldron on the fire. She picks up the ladle and begins, slowly, to stir.

Something else in the village is stirring—the children. It seems like all the children in all the houses have sensed the presence of this traveler. They peek through the blinds. They whisper to their siblings. Finally, they can't take it anymore. Locks are snapped back, doors are flung open, and kids from across this village come flying through their doors into the town square.

They gather around the woman, a little scared at first, but feeling more and more comfortable as the minutes go by. Soon enough, some adults emerge. They pretend that they are just there to look after the children, but the truth is they are a little curious too.

Finally, one of the kids asks, "What are you doing?"

The woman looks up from stirring the pot, smiles, and says, "Why, I'm making stone soup." She picks up the stone that has been lying by her side and places it in the cauldron.

It takes a few minutes for one of the teenagers to work up the courage to say, "Listen, we're all hungry. Is it going to be done soon?"

The woman smiles and says, "Yes, of course. It's almost there. It just needs some carrots."

One of the adults pipes up, "We've got carrots." Everybody turns to stare. There's food in the village after all? The man has surprised himself with how quickly and publicly he made his announcement. He stands up and walks toward his home, locates the carrots where he has hidden them away, and returns.

The woman chops up the carrots, slides them into the stone soup, and keeps stirring.

Soon enough someone else asks, "Well, is it ready now?"

"Mmmmm," she says, "almost. Just needs some potatoes."

"We've got potatoes!" says a voice from the crowd.

The pattern repeats itself. The soup is not quite done until every household in the village has made a contribution. Turns out that the inhabitants had more than they knew—some people had vegetables, others had bread. Silverware and dishes appeared, as did tables and chairs.

Soon enough, the village is feasting—with the resources that they had all along. And none of it would have happened without the traveler.

So what did she do that was so remarkable?

Well, the first thing she did was have a vision. She saw a starving village and imagined a community. Marcel Proust says, "The true journey of discovery is not in seeing new landscapes but in developing new eyes."[10]

The second thing she did was to see people's assets, not their deficits. She just had a feeling that every inhabitant in the village had a contribution to make, and that, if the space was right, those contributions might go well together.

Finally, she organized a concrete activity that created the right space. Note the central importance of the activity. She didn't simply roll into the village and shout, "Hey you idiots, don't you know that if you figured out a way to share the food you're each hiding you could create a feast and you wouldn't be starving?" Instead, she created what amounted to a game to nudge each of them to bring their offering, contribute to a collective feast, and create a sense of community.

Right now, America is like that divided village. People are isolated, scared of one another, either refusing to listen or unable to find the words to communicate.

Truth be told, our diversity is likely contributing to this division. In his paper "E Pluribus Unum: Diversity and Community in the Twenty-First Century," Robert Putnam reported that an increase in diversity in a community leads to a decrease in social trust. Diversity, he pointed out, needs to be positively and proactively engaged for it to build community.[11] That's why leaders who have the vision, knowledge, and skills to build the kind of spaces represented by the Stone

Soup story are so crucial. We need more such people: Leaders who know that, with the right format and activity, people can be nudged to deemphasize their disagreements and center the things they have in common. Leaders who have the courage to take the initiative and create those activities.

In a diverse democracy, if the people don't contribute, the community doesn't feast.

Real-life versions of this mythical potluck actually exist in contemporary America. In a previous chapter, I wrote about the People's Supper, created by Lennon Flowers and Jen Bailey. But I also love the model created by Questlove, the drummer for The Roots. He calls his version "mixtape potlucks." Using his proclivities as a musician, he sends out a song to each of the people he's inviting and asks them to bring a dish that the song inspires. In an NPR interview about these gatherings, Questlove describes himself as a loner by nature ("Rapunzel with an afro," is his memorable turn of phrase) who discovered an inner potluck host that he didn't previously know existed.[12]

JANE ADDAMS: CIVIC INSTITUTIONS AND SOCIAL CHANGE

Can civic institutions at the local level lead to social change at the national level? It has happened before, in an era with remarkable similarities to ours.

I refer to the turn of the twentieth century. Immigration was profoundly changing the ethnic and religious makeup of the nation. A massive economic shift was taking place as industrialization overtook the agrarian economy. Great wealth was being made in some quarters and there was devastating poverty in others, creating an ugly income inequality. Cities grew rapidly and were, for many people, horribly unsanitary and dangerous places to live. Labor conditions were even worse. A communications revolution was underway, with the invention of both the radio and the telephone, and racist hate groups were on the rise.

Into this maelstrom Jane Addams came with an ethic not unlike the one that drove Jen and Lennon to create the People's Supper. In 1889, Addams started an institution called Hull House on the near West Side of Chicago whose initial purpose was to meet the immediate needs of, and create community among, the diverse array of immigrants in the Nineteenth Ward. She died there nearly a half century later, having built what many consider the best example of democracy in action that America has ever seen.

She started by making concrete and positive improvements for the local community. Hull House leaders—almost all women—were pioneers in urban sociology. Their research mapped the ethnic makeup of the Nineteenth Ward of Chicago and highlighted many of the problems there as well. They learned that there were seven thousand school age children in the ward, but only three thousand seats in the local public school.[13] So Hull House organized classes and activities for kids. There were hundreds of residents in the blocks west of Hull House, but only three bathtubs. So Hull House built public baths.

For virtually every problem that they discovered in Chicago, they modeled a concrete solution. Many of these initiatives flew in the face of conventional wisdom, otherwise known as the prejudices of the time.

Think that young people are simply ticking time bombs of trouble waiting to explode? Come see the Boy Scout group and other youth leadership programs at Hull House.

You think that saloons are the only place that people will gather? Come hang out at the coffee shop we built at Hull House.

You feel that high culture and advanced education should only be reserved for certain ethnic groups and social classes? Come participate in the book groups, art workshops, and college extension courses at Hull House.

You think tensions between Protestants, Catholics, and Jews are inevitable? Well, Hull House is a self-consciously interfaith space organized around "the fellowship of the deed." Come see how well things turn out when people from different religions work together.

You think that diversity requires separation? Come see how tasty the food is at the public kitchen at Hull House, where people from different nations share traditional recipes and prepare delicious meals.

You don't believe that women have the intellectual ability to vote? Well, come see who runs things at Hull House.

Hull House was democracy in action. John Dewey visited, often. His daughter later said that these visits profoundly deepened his understanding of the possibility of America, an influence that found its way into Dewey's writings about democracy.[14]

Another great pragmatist philosopher, William James, once wrote Jane Addams a letter with the line: "The fact is, Madam, that you are not like the rest of us, who *seek* the truth and *try* to express it. *You inhabit* reality; and when you open your mouth truth can't help being uttered."[15]

But while Jane Addams might have started with building concrete solutions to local problems, she didn't end there. Instead, she used Hull House as a model for remarkable citywide and national reform movements. Walter Isaacson once said that Steve Jobs transformed seven industries—personal computing, animated movies, retail, music, phones, digital publishing, and tablets.[16] Jane Addams transformed at least as many areas of American democracy.

From her base at Hull House, she fought for women's suffrage, protested against war, helped found the NAACP, and was a key leader of the ACLU. She recognized the power and possibility of the newly emerging category of adolescence. She wrote articles against lynching and was friends with the famed Black feminist Ida B. Wells-Barnett. She stood up for the politically unpopular while still working with politicians, was seen as fair-minded enough by both CEOs and union leaders to mediate labor disputes, and launched investigations into diseases that led to new laws and government agencies that dramatically improved public health.

Jane Addams expanded the definition of American democracy and of American citizenship. Racist movements tried to keep new immigrants out. Jane Addams looked at them, and American democracy, differently. These new arrivals were necessary contributors, not strangers. Indeed, America wasn't truly a democracy if it would not dignify the identities and invite the contributions of all its varied people. She wrote: "The good we secure for ourselves is precarious and uncertain until it is secured for all of us and incorporated into our common life."[17]

That included people with views and identities different from your own. Addams wrote, "We know instinctively that if we grow contemptuous of our fellows and consciously limit our intercourse to certain kinds of people whom we have previously decided to respect, we not only circumscribe our range of life but limit the scope of our ethics."[18]

All of this might seem obvious now, but it wasn't at the time, and that is part of Jane Addams's achievement. She built a full layer of American democracy that we now take entirely for granted.

Jane Addams was clearly willing to critique when she felt the circumstances called for it—she very publicly opposed World War I—but she didn't put much stock in being ideologically pure. In the best pragmatist tradition, she did the right thing according to the circumstance and the evidence, always with the twin purpose of helping the most vulnerable people in the here and now, and strengthening American democracy over the long haul.

In other words, she was a builder.

We know a great deal about Jane Addams's personal journey. And lo and behold, it has profound similarities to the path that a lot of young social change agents walk today.

Books and travel expanded her horizons, but they didn't answer the deeper existential questions. She fell into a depression, a condition that doctors at the time referred to as neurasthenia.

What brought her out of it? She found what she wanted to build.

On a visit to the East End of London, she witnessed a scene that made a profound impression upon her. A man stood in the midst of a crowd of poor people, holding aloft rotting vegetables, contemptuously inviting the laborers to bid on a meager dinner. When one worker gave his day's wages for a cabbage, it was flung at him. Jane

Addams watched as the famished man sat on the ground and tore into the spoiled vegetable, unwashed and uncooked.

The moment reminded Jane Addams of a dream that she had as a little girl: the world needed saving and she wanted to play her role, so she built a wagon wheel.

What could she build now that she was a college-educated young woman witnessing firsthand the suffering so many were enduring at a time of tectonic social and economic change, while herself experiencing a kind of aimlessness that had descended into depression?

The answer to that turned out to be Hull House. It started off as a way to meet the needs of recent immigrant laborers and their children in a part of the city that people like Jane Addams were not supposed to go. It turned into a way to renew American democracy.

Frederick Buechner has a classic line about vocation. He uses religious language: "The place God calls you to is the place where your deep gladness and the world's deep hunger meet."[19]

For Jane Addams that place had an address—800 South Halsted. She lived there from 1889 until her death in 1935. That's finding your calling.

And she started off, as she later wrote in *Twenty Years at Hull House*, as a young person seeking, "To construct the world anew and conform it to (my) own ideals."

CHAPTER SIX

THE OBAMA STORY, THE TRUMP STORY

O N VIRTUALLY EVERY DAY SINCE DONALD TRUMP DECLARED his candidacy for president, virtually every publication I read ran an article on one Trump outrage or another. At some point, they all took to keeping a kind of catalogue of Trump outrages.

Midway through Trump's presidency, *The Atlantic* published a list of his top fifty most unthinkable moments. "He is a demagogue, a xenophobe, a sexist, a know-nothing, and a liar," it stated, by way of summary. Jeffrey Goldberg, *The Atlantic*'s editor-in-chief, later said that the magazine "may be guilty of understatement."[1]

The *New York Times* dedicated their *entire* ten-page "Week in Review" section on Sunday, October 18, 2020, to what they called "The Case Against Donald Trump."[2] The *Washington Post* kept a regularly updated journal of his false and misleading claims.[3]

The accumulation of all of this has something of a numbing effect, in a "one dead is a tragedy, a million deaths is a statistic" kind of way. I cherish my sanity, so I switched the television news off more than once when the subject turned to Donald Trump. I literally used my morning prayer and meditation to try to cleanse his presence from my being. But there is one piece of tape featuring Donald Trump that I cannot remove from my mind. On any objective scale, it would probably not make a list of Trump's top one thousand outrages. In fact, neither Donald Trump's voice nor his person make a direct appearance. And yet the tape plays over and over in my mind. It haunts me, and in a strange way it has come to symbolize for me the way that the Trump story has deformed this nation.

The video is all of eight seconds long. It is grainy and jumpy, shot on a cell phone in a middle school lunchroom in Royal Oak, Michigan, on the day after Trump was elected in 2016. The viewer sees a gaggle of skinny boys and girls, dressed in shorts and T-shirts, sitting at plastic cafeteria tables. The faces have been blurred, but the chant rings out loud and clear: "Build the wall, build the wall, build the wall." News reports claimed that it was directed at a small group of Hispanic students in the cafeteria.[4] Royal Oak has just under sixty thousand residents, and over fifty thousand of them are white.

I cannot stop watching the video, even though it gives me nightmares. And I cannot make out who the Hispanic kids are. I really wish I could. I wish I could see the looks on their faces. It might give me a bit of closure on the whole sequence. Instead, that part is left to my imagination. Are there tears swimming in their eyes, or are they winning that fight? Does it seem like they have endured months of such torment, or is this the first time? Are they being comforted and supported by an adult? Or are their teachers the types who might have attended a Trump rally and chanted the slogan themselves?

And then comes the flood of memories. The dozens of times that racist chants were directed my way in a 90 percent–white middle school cafeteria in the western suburbs of Chicago in the late 1980s. "Hindoo, Hindoo, Hindoo," the kids would say as I sat alone in a corner of the lunchroom, wishing I could die or disappear. There is something deeply chilling about the sound of a racist chant in the voices of prepubescent youth. Hell is a middle school lunchroom.

The pack always had a leader. A kid who saw me trying to sneak by unnoticed, who directed the attention of the crowd, who changed the conversation from football or parties to me, who handed around stones in the form of a racist chant.

Seventh grade for me was seven hours a day, five days a week of putting on an emotional armor and trying to power through school. It was steeling myself every morning to win the fight to hold back tears. I remember trying to tell my parents once, and them just not getting it. "Hinduism is a religion," my mother said, confused. "There are so many great people who are Hindus. Gandhi, Vivekananda. So many of my friends growing up in India were Hindu."

She just could not understand how it would be hurled as a slur. I stopped trying to explain. How could I? I didn't understand it myself.

But here is what I did understand. I was done being a target. The way out? Well, I had become expert in the methods of racist bullies. All I needed was an opening.

The summer after I graduated from eighth grade, my cousin from Mumbai came to visit. She was a few years older and desperately in need of friends. My mom enrolled us both in a computer class at the community college where she taught accounting. She viewed it as an opportunity for us to climb a few rungs up the ladder of meritocracy. My cousin was hoping to make friends. I had a whole different ambition.

As we walked to class on the first day, I said I needed to use the restroom and told her to go on ahead. "Remember," she said, perhaps intuiting what I was about to do, "you are the only person I know here."

I ducked into the bathroom, waited five minutes, then headed for the class. I avoided her eyes as I walked in and chose a seat as far away from her as possible. I could feel her staring forlornly at me.

The professor had us go around the room and introduce ourselves. My cousin's thick Indian accent marked her immediately, just like I knew it would. I heard a couple of students chortle and saw my cousin wince ever so slightly. She had heard it too. The white frat guy next to me leaned over and said, "When do you think she got off the boat?"

"Her hair is even worse than her accent," I retorted. He laughed out loud, and right then I knew that my plan had worked. I knew exactly how racial lines operated. I, who had so often been cast on the dark side, had found a way into the white. All I needed to do was identify the fully grown version of the racist ringleader in the middle school cafeteria and be his accomplice in targeting someone else.

I think my cousin could tell that something was going on. I mean, I wasn't trying to be subtle. We were constantly laughing and making gestures in her direction. I knew exactly what to do. I used every racist taunt and joke that was ever targeted at me against her. Slurpee maker. Dothead. Camel jockey. And I was even more expert in fitting in, having watched other kids do it with intense jealousy. I could not turn my skin white, but I could wear the same heavy metal T-shirts my new frat boy friend wore, I could copy his mannerisms, and most of all, I could outdo him in wielding the weapon of racism.

And what was that weapon? It was not a sharp object. It was not a gun or a bomb. It was a story. And it was made lethal because the person next to me, on account of his authority in the culture, had power. And by allying myself with him, I had power too.

I cannot begin to tell you the surge of strength that I felt every day in class, sitting next to him, slinging my stones across the room. It was matched only in intensity by the shame that came over me as I walked back to the car with my cousin, watching her face contort as she fought back tears. I knew exactly what was going on in her head: should she confront me, or pretend like she didn't care? I had flipped back and forth between those options in my mind a million times. Except this time I was the cause of the suffering, not the one suffering myself.

When I look back at that summer, I cannot believe that I had such vileness inside me. But I suppose we all do. The vileness competes with the goodness inside all of us. The question is which dimension comes to the surface. The great writer Zadie Smith once said,

> Individual citizens are internally plural. They have within them the full range of behavioral possibilities. They are like complex musical scores from which certain melodies can be teased out and others ignored or suppressed, depending, at least in part, on who

is doing the conducting. At this moment, all over the world—and most recently in America—the conductors standing in front of this human orchestra have only the meanest and most banal melodies in mind.[5]

The metaphor of a conductor is almost too kind for Donald Trump. I think of him more like the evil wizard Saruman, from *The Lord of the Rings*, using the powers of story to bring out the orc in tens of millions of people, forming them into a political force that, for four years, crowded out the light.

Whatever power white frat boy types might have held in my world when I was in middle school, it is a speck of dust in comparison to the power that is held by the president of the United States. So I can only imagine the surge of strength that middle schoolers experienced when they were handed a simple slogan like Build the Wall and an obvious target.

You see, the wall is not simply a structure. Building it is not just an immigration policy. The wall is a story. It is a story about who belongs in America and who doesn't, about who gets to speak and who has to steel themselves against racist attacks every day while going to school.

One wonders what story those seventh graders in that cafeteria in Royal Oak, Michigan, might have told about the diversity of their lunchroom had they been presented with a different leader, someone who elevated them rather than invited them to degrade their classmates. And also, what corrosion was happening in their own souls as they followed the leader they were given. James Baldwin wrote that racism was not just a prison for the people of color who are its targets but also for the white people who believed it gave them power. It was making them "criminals and monsters."[6] You cannot degrade another human being without degrading yourself.

"The stories we fall in love with make us who we are," writes Salman Rushdie. He continues: "The beloved tale becomes a part of the way we understand things and make judgments and choices in our daily lives."[7]

If you are a child and someone arms you with a story that gives you power by breaking others, it makes sense that you use it to divide your middle school lunchroom between the white kids who form the inner circle and the brown kids who are excluded.

Stories form the social DNA of individual human beings, and also entire nations. What is a nation, after all, but a collection of stories that builds toward a collective solidarity? An "agreed-upon past," in the words of Jill Lepore, that makes a mass of individuals, most of whom will never meet, still feel connected enough that they cherish the same ideals, consent to the same laws, and, if necessary, are willing to go to war for one another.[8]

"What unites this country," writes the philosopher Kwame Anthony Appiah, "is not that we are all the same but rather that so many of us think of America as ours. That sense of possession comes from our belief that we each have a place in a great national narrative that only we are a part of and whose complete story none of us knows because we are each only aware of a part of it."[9]

If we are to have a common life together, we will have to tell stories that connect us to each other across identities, that give us a sense of pride in one another's thriving.

America has had no shortage of Donald Trumps, willing to wield a story as a weapon to break and divide. But we have also had a plethora of figures who have helped us fall in love with more beautiful stories, bridging narratives, not breaking them. Leaders who, to borrow from Zadie Smith, "play . . . a finer music," and are adept at "encouraging others . . . to sing along."[10]

OBAMA AS HOOPOE

I remember the first time I heard the name Barack Obama. It was 2002 and I had just returned to Chicago from graduate school in England intent on starting Interfaith America. Toward that end, I made a list of prominent Chicagoans who I thought could help me.

Mayor Daley was first on my list. Cardinal George was second. The great historian of American religion, Martin Marty, was third. CEOs of major companies and presidents of large philanthropic foundations rounded out the top ten. Somebody told me, "You should meet this guy Barack Obama. He'd love the idea of an interfaith youth organization. He's just a local politician now, but wait until America finds out about him—he's going to be something big."

I looked Obama up online. The most relevant piece of information seemed to be that he'd lost a congressional race to a former Black Panther, Bobby Rush, by some thirty points.[11] That didn't strike me as the résumé of someone moving fast up the food chain. Obama made my list at number forty-three. I never got down that far.

I shake my head when I think about that now. The man who would become the most powerful person in the world in 2008 was, less than a decade before, virtually unknown even in his own city. How did he do it? By telling a story that convinced Americans that ours was a nation that makes a virtue of talking to strangers, engaging with opponents, and expanding the circle of inclusion.

The cornerstone of the Obama narrative is that everybody belongs, that their being has been given its original, unshakeable dignity by God, and that America, at its best, expresses that divine love by making sure we matter to each other. In his address at the 2004 Democratic National Convention, Obama spoke of children on the South Side of Chicago who couldn't read, senior citizens who had to choose between rent and medicine, Arab American families worried about being rounded up by government officials on suspicion of terrorism. Being American means that all of these people matter, that their problems are everyone's problems, that their hopes and their potential inspire all of us, indeed define who we are. "It's that fundamental belief—I am my brother's keeper, I am my sister's keeper—that makes this country work. It's what allows us to pursue our individual dreams, yet still come together as a single American family."[12]

For Obama, America's politics should be as idealistic as our highest principles and as decent as our civic spaces. Again, from his 2004

Democratic Convention address: "The pundits like to slice-and-dice our country into . . . Red States for Republicans, Blue States for Democrats. But I've got news for them. We worship an awesome God in the Blue States, and we don't like federal agents poking around our libraries in the Red States. We coach Little League in the Blue States, and have gay friends in the Red States."

For Obama, our nation's diversity is America's greatest asset. He spoke of our "patchwork heritage as a strength not a weakness," of a nation "shaped by every language and culture" who, precisely because of the combination of our history of ugly conflicts and inspiring social movements, might "play its role in ushering in a new era of peace."[13]

But he also cautioned against identity being wielded as a bunker of isolation, a barrier of division, or a bludgeon of domination. He was concerned about people canceling one another based on disagreements, worried about the general retreat from democratic discourse. In the Obama narrative, America was about diverse people empathizing with each other's struggles, and realizing that we rise and fall together. Here is how he put it in his farewell address:

> For blacks and other minorities (advocating for change), it means tying our own struggles for justice to the challenges that a lot of people in this country face—the refugee, the immigrant, the rural poor, the transgender American, and also the middle-aged white man who from the outside may seem like he's got all the advantages, but who's seen his world upended by economic, cultural, and technological change. . . . Democracy does require a basic sense of solidarity—the idea that for all our outward differences, we are all in this together; that we rise or fall as one.[14]

In the Obama narrative, America was about bridges—bridges that linked us to each other and bridges that connected all of us to a more inclusive future. He recognized that living in a diverse democracy means we are going to disagree with people on some fundamental things and we need to keep working with them on others. He sought common ground amidst deep differences and civility when discussing irreconcilable disagreements. Obama wasn't going to buy a brownie from the KKK bake sale, but he was going to engage positively with virtually everyone else.

My favorite example of this was when Obama was invited to give the commencement address at Notre Dame University and receive an honorary degree. Thousands of pro-life activists came to South Bend to protest a Catholic university honoring a pro-choice president. The demonstrations received wall-to-wall coverage on cable news. It's become commonplace for high-profile people to withdraw from commencement addresses when a whiff of controversy emerges. Obama did not. He went to Notre Dame, was gracious when pro-life demonstrators interrupted his address, and proceeded to relate the story of a letter he'd received from a doctor when he was running for the Senate in 2004. The doctor was pro-life, but he was not writing to ask Obama to change his position on abortion. Instead, he was concerned that the Obama for Senate website promised to "fight right-wing ideologues who want to take away a woman's right to choose." The doctor was concerned about the distorted picture Obama was painting of people who held opposing convictions on a serious matter and simply asked him to represent people with whom he disagreed in "fair-minded words."

Obama agreed. He apologized to the doctor who had written him the letter, and he instructed his staff to change the language on the website.

Standing on the commencement stage at Notre Dame, Obama ran down a familiar litany of common ground ways that the pro-life and pro-choice camps might work together to reduce abortion—reducing unwanted pregnancies, encouraging adoption—all of which earned applause from the audience. But he didn't avoid the hard part. Instead, he said, "no matter how much we may want to fudge it . . . the fact is that at some level, the views of the two camps are irreconcilable. Each side will continue to make its case to the public with passion and conviction. But surely we can do so without reducing those with differing views to caricature."

And then Obama said that it was *pro-life Catholics who had taught him this lesson*. There were the Catholics he had worked with as a community organizer on the South Side of Chicago, when he was not much older than the graduates in that building. The Catholic sisters, some of the most Christ-like people that he knew. And then there were the Catholic intellectuals who had given him the philosophical language to describe the type of diversity work he decided he wanted to exemplify. He quoted one of those intellectuals—Father Ted Hesburgh, the man who had served as president of Notre Dame for some fifty years, growing it from a modest Catholic institution to a major research university—and who was in the audience that day: "Father Hesburgh has long spoken of this institution as both a lighthouse and a crossroads. A lighthouse that stands apart, shining with the wisdom of the Catholic tradition, while the crossroads is where 'differences of culture and religion and conviction can co-exist with friendship, civility, hospitality, and especially love.'"[15]

One of the things I love about Obama is the way he wove the pragmatic and the sacred together. Like Lincoln, Obama spoke often of his belief in God and his belief in American democracy in the same breath. And like Lincoln, he believed that expanding the circle to include people of all identities, including a variety of religious identities, was of cosmic significance. He spoke about America being a nation of many religions in his inaugural address, and I experienced his personal commitment to the issue as a member of his Inaugural Faith Council, working with him to launch the President's Interfaith Challenge.

As a Christian, Obama's religious language is derived largely from the Bible. As a Muslim, I saw him fulfilling a role that is familiar to anyone who knows Sufi poetry.

I speak of Farid ud-Din Attar's medieval Muslim masterpiece *The Conference of the Birds*. The story begins with the birds complaining that they, of all the species, do not have a king. Every other species seems to know its master, save the poor, bereft birds.

One bird, the hoopoe, speaks up. Actually, the birds do have a king. His name is the great Simurgh. The birds are thrilled—that is, until the hoopoe points out that the Simurgh resides far away and can only be reached after an arduous journey crossing seven mountains and seven valleys.

Suddenly, the birds are no longer interested in seeing the Simurgh. One by one, they begin to make excuses about why they can't travel, or why it wasn't so important to begin with. The reader gets the sense that some of these birds would rather they did not have the knowledge of the Simurgh. They'd prefer to complain about the situation than to know that it can be rectified with the right amount of effort.

The hoopoe is not giving up that easily. He goes bird by bird, telling each of them an individual story about what she will receive from making the journey.

Finally, a group of birds is ready to travel. They are led by the hoopoe across the seven mountains and valleys toward the land of the great Simurgh. The entire way, the birds are encouraged by the storytelling of the hoopoe.

Ultimately, they arrive at the court of the great Simurgh. They announce themselves and are admitted. When they enter, they are greeted by a beautiful shimmering lake, in which they see their own reflections. "*Simurgh*," in Persian, means "thirty birds."

For me, the point of the story is clear and powerful: a diverse community that undertakes an arduous journey, commits to themselves and each other, is its own king, its own form of holiness. It is the American experiment in a nutshell, and it underscores that our attempt at being a diverse democracy is not just a civic project but also a sacred one.

During his years on the national stage, Obama played the role of hoopoe, encouraging, cajoling, pointing forward, telling a story that made all of us feel as if we were on a journey and, by traveling together, becoming our own king.

Obama was well aware of the power of story; in fact he spoke about it explicitly. In a 2018 address in South Africa, commemorating what would have been the hundredth birthday of Nelson Mandela, Obama said that the world stood at a crossroads between two great stories. There was the story of fear and division on the one hand and the story of common hopes and common dreams on the other. With the rise of Trump and other nationalist leaders like Narendra Modi in India, Viktor Orbán in Hungary, Benjamin Netanyahu in Israel, and Recep Tayyip Erdoğan in Turkey, it seemed like the fear and division story was winning. But Obama felt that was only temporary. Progressives who believed in multicultural participatory democracies had a better story to tell. And even in this dark hour, we should feel confident about singing our song and shining our light.

There was no better symbol of that story than Nelson Mandela. Obama reminded us that Mandela was fond of saying that not only did hate have to be taught; it was also actually a hard lesson to learn, because "love comes more naturally to the human heart." On the subject of love for others, Nelson Mandela achieved mastery. He did not hate his jailers at Robben Island, and not just because he refused to give them the satisfaction of both imprisoning his body and distorting his mind. It was because he wanted them to be better people, and he knew it was ennobling to play a role in that process. So Mandela learned their language, listened to stories of their children even when he could not see his own, invited some to stand with him when he was inaugurated as president of the country. He wore the jersey of the favorite sports team of apartheid-supporting white South Africans—the Springboks—and by doing so he transformed the meaning of that jersey from a symbol of racist oppression to a symbol of a multicultural nation. He spoke of working with the enemy in such a way that that enemy could not help but become a partner in the doing of good. Obama characterized it in this way: "The subjugator was being offered a gift, being given a chance to see in a new way, being given a chance to participate in the work of building a better world."[16]

While Obama had never endured anything close to what Mandela had suffered, both men had in common something exceedingly rare—they began their work in progressive activist circles and climbed to the heights of political power.

As is well known, Obama arrived in Chicago in his early twenties to be a community organizer. His interpretation of that role in those formative years was to cast himself as an agitator in the face of those with power. After a while, Obama thought to himself, *Why am I always protesting against the political leaders? Why not try to be the political leader and make what I think are the right decisions from a position of governing, not criticizing?*

As his national profile grew, it was clear that Obama had learned a deeper lesson from his years as an organizer: power wasn't just something you had to oppose, it was something you had to seek, and wield responsibly. That meant engaging with everyone—the people who agreed with you and the people who didn't.

As a community organizer, Obama was no doubt familiar with Saul Alinsky's book *Rules for Radicals*, the classic text of the field. In the prologue, Alinsky offers this counsel: *view the people with whom you disagree as your constituents.* Imagine yourself a leader who is responsible for the thriving of people with whom you identify and also with the thriving of people with whom you don't. Ask yourself: What's the best way to communicate with them? What language should I speak to maximize the chances that I am understood?

Before any social change takes place in a nation, Alinsky emphasizes, an internal change has to take place within the people. That requires the change agent to work within other people's framework of experience, not *their own* preferred mode of self-expression. Don't walk into an Orthodox Jewish neighborhood eating a ham sandwich unless you want to be thrown out on your ear, however much you might like ham.

This is the world as it is—and you have no choice but to start from it. The alternative, Alinsky says, is to have no voice at all, which is simply another way of saying that you have voted for the status quo.

Working to persuade people of your vision means working within the system of democratic norms and processes. Be grateful for fundamentals like free speech, civil discourse, and (generally) open elections. Such fundamentals don't exist in other nations, and you would most certainly miss them if they disappeared. Recognizing that the American system itself allows for social change agents to make their case, and agreeing to work within this system, is what Alinsky calls "radical pragmatism."[17]

Obama, for all of his cosmic storytelling, is very much a radical pragmatist. He knew that the ideals that are stated in soaring narratives do not magically shape themselves into a strong social infrastructure. Governing is more than storytelling. It's not just the protests that we participate in or the speeches that we give, he told his audience in South Africa. "It's also about the civic culture that we build that makes democracy work." If we are going to realize the dream of creating a healthy diverse democracy, Obama said, "we're going to have to innovate . . . we're going to have to build."[18]

CHAPTER SEVEN

THE GENIUS OF
RELIGIOUS INSTITUTIONS

WHAT WOULD HAPPEN IF ALL THE HOUSES OF WORSHIP IN your neighborhood disappeared tomorrow? Of course, this would be a tragedy for worshippers, who would not have a place to have their spirits tended. But the social consequences would be at least as devastating as the spiritual ones. Where would the local Alcoholics Anonymous group meet? Who would organize volunteers to go visit the senior center? What would happen to all the families who rely on the food served in the soup kitchens?

Now imagine not just the congregations in your town disappearing but also all of the institutions that were founded by religious traditions. You may not have that many hospitals left. Some of the best in my city—Northwestern, Rush, Loyola—were founded, respectively, by Methodists, Presbyterians, and Jesuits. You'd certainly have fewer colleges and K–12 schools. The Y would be gone—after all, the original name was the Young Men's Christian Association, or YMCA. A good number of the social service agencies in your community would disappear as well. Catholic Charities likely supports something like half of them, and many of the rest—homeless shelters, soup kitchens, legal aid, adoption services—were no doubt founded by a range of other religious communities. And what would happen in case of a disaster? The Southern Baptists run one of the largest disaster relief agencies in the country. And think of all the kids who enjoy overnight summer camp. They would likely be staying home, as many of those camps were started by religious groups.

Throughout this book, I have defined a strategic institution as one that instantiates ideals through a web of concrete programs. At their best, religions are a network of institutions that seek to make real an inspiring vision that adherents believe was set forth by God, a vision that makes everyone sacred. The Church is the mystical body of Christ, organizing itself such that it engages the world the way Jesus would. Jewish institutions are called to be the arms and legs of God on Earth. Islam is not just about ritual prayer and doctrinal beliefs; it is equally about how human beings treat other human beings. This horizontal relationship between humans is connected to our vertical relationship with God. The tradition of primacy, meaning the first lesson that classical Muslim scholars taught their students, went like this: *The One in heaven is merciful. If you are merciful to others, He will be merciful to you.*

This chapter is about what we can learn from the vision, impact, and durability of religious communities, which are amongst the oldest social institutions that we humans have created and maintained.

When I was in college, attempting to carve out a space for myself as the resident radical on all subjects, I found myself in a searching conversation with a group of fellow students on the topic of religion. People were sharing faith journeys, spiritual practices that gave them meaning, stories of family traditions related to religious rituals. At the time, I hadn't thought about religion very much at all, but I was desperate for my voice to be heard, so I said something that makes me want to cover my face with shame when I think about it today. In a tone that took flippancy and scorn to new heights, I said that religion seemed like one big fraud to me, and if the Catholic Church practiced what it preached, it would start a bunch of schools and hospitals.

After a brief silence, someone sitting at the table said, "That's exactly what the Church did."

How could I say something so utterly foolish in public? Around the world, the Catholic Church runs 5,500 hospitals, 18,000 health clinics, and 16,000 homes for the elderly and those with special needs. In the United States alone, there are 230 Catholic colleges and universities and thousands of K–12 schools. It would be impossible to count all the soup kitchens, homeless shelters, counseling programs, and other contributions to the social infrastructure performed by the 200,000 Catholic parishes around the globe. The Catholic Church, quite simply, is the world's largest charitable organization.[1]

Here's the kicker: virtually my entire family has benefited from such institutions. In the mid-1970s, a university started by French Catholic priests alongside a beautiful lake in central Indiana found fit to admit a somewhat wayward Ismaili Muslim from India to its MBA program. That man was my father, and that is the short version of how I came to be in this country (and also how I wound up a rabid fan of Fighting Irish football).

My mother went to Catholic school as a girl in Mumbai and has her master's degree from a Catholic university in the United States, DePaul. My wife went to a Catholic law school, Loyola University, and both of my kids went to Catholic preschools. All of us, at one time or another, have been treated at hospitals built by Catholics.

The Catholic Church is unique in scale, but not in kind. In their book *The Upswing*, Robert Putnam and Shaylyn Romney Garrett write, "Religious institutions have long been the single most important source of community connectedness and social solidarity in America. Even in our secular age, roughly half of all group memberships are religious in nature—congregations, Bible study groups, prayer circles, and so forth—and roughly half of all philanthropy and volunteering is carried out in a religious context."[2]

Here is how Putnam puts it in his earlier work, *Bowling Alone*: "[religious communities] provide an important incubator for civic skills, civic norms, community interests and civic recruitment. Religiously active men and women learn to give speeches, run meetings, manage disagreements and bear administrative responsibility."[3] As proof, he lists the programs on the calendar of a single day at Riverside Church on the Upper West Side of Manhattan. The activities included everything from meetings of the Ecology Task Force and the Narcotics Anonymous group to trainings for the staff of various social service programs to martial arts classes.

Importantly, that civic energy doesn't stay within the confines of the religious community; it gets offered to the broader society. People who join the Ecology Task Force at Riverside Church might find themselves being asked to lead a meeting, then being elected to chair the Task Force, and then deciding to start a similar Ecology Task Force in their workplace or neighborhood. Putnam and Romney Garrett report that people who are active in religious communities "are more than twice as likely to volunteer as demographically matched Americans who rarely attend church, and to volunteer not merely for church ushering, but also for secular causes." Moreover, they make a claim to something that social scientists are generally enormously cautious about: "the link between religious involvement and civic do-gooding is not spurious, but probably causal."

Americans remain remarkably religious in comparison to citizens of other industrialized nations, but our involvement with religious communities has fallen dramatically. Congregations virtually across the board are losing participants. In their book *American Grace*, Robert Putnam and David Campbell note that involvement in religious communities has always had ups and downs in American history.[4] It hit a high point in the 1950s, then a low point in the 1960s, then rose again in the 1970s and 1980s. As I write, religious involvement is at another low, and it is having a deep impact on the types of civic institutions that religious communities establish. The Southern Baptist denomination has trained eighty thousand people in disaster relief. They are on the ground within twenty-four hours of a tornado or a hurricane, doing everything from cleaning debris to helping people find shelter to preparing food. And it's not just the Southern Baptists. Over half of the members of the National Voluntary Organizations Active in Disaster are faith-based groups—Catholics, Methodists, Buddhists, Lutherans, Latter-day Saints, Muslims. It is interfaith America in action.

But as the numbers of people involved in those religious communities decline, so does the strength of faith-based agencies. There are fewer volunteers, less money, lower morale. Brad Fulton, an associate professor of nonprofit management at Indiana University, doesn't have any problem with the philosophy of being spiritual but not religious when it comes to individuals. It's not saving souls that he is principally concerned with. But he is worried about what happens to the social infrastructure of our society if American religious belonging continues to decline. He says, "There is some upside to organized religion that has very little to do with religion. They have a great mechanism to bring people together."[5]

In my view, there is absolutely reason for concern, but there is also cause for hope. Part of the genius of faith communities is how they adapt to changing times. Consider, for example, the chapel car, an innovation of nineteenth-century frontier America, a time when Americans were moving West (too often terrorizing and displacing Indigenous people in the process) to settle land and build new lives. There were of course no Christian churches on the frontier, so clergy, both Protestant and Catholic, seeking an innovative way to reach the unchurched, began to outfit train cars as mini-chapels and brought Christianity to the settlers on the frontier.[6]

It is precisely this creativity that has made the institutions of religion perhaps the most durable institutions we know. Durable does not mean unchanging. Durable means long lasting, which suggests the ability to alter forms to achieve mission.

Another part of the effectiveness of religious institutions is the manner in which they have worked themselves into the collective consciousness, providing a structure for a range of endeavors. Take, for example, my avowedly secular friend Eric Liu. While not a believer in God, Eric realizes the deep wisdom and power in religion and has looked to faith traditions for inspiration on how to structure the programs of his organization, Citizen University.

The mission of Citizen University is to foster a culture of powerful citizenship in the United States. The central initiative is a Civic Saturday, in which Eric and his cofounder and wife, Jena, lead a gathering through the arc of what feels very much like a religious worship service. They stand and read aloud from a variety of "sacred civic texts" (from the Declaration of Independence to the Declaration of Sentiments), they sing songs and recite poems, they listen to a civic sermon, they turn to one another and offer greetings of peace and pledges of solidarity.

Eric fully admits that he borrowed the model from religion, wholesale. In his wonderful book *Become America*, he writes, "Why the analogy to faith gatherings? In part because over the millennia major faiths have figured out something about how to help people find meaning and belonging, how to interpret texts and to reckon with the gap between our ideals and our reality, how to sustain hope and heart in a sea of cynicism and hate."[7]

Democracy in America, Eric insists, is also an act of faith. Like religious traditions, American civic religion has sacred texts and powerful rituals, like swearing-in ceremonies for new citizens. Most of all, a self-governing diverse democracy requires people to have profound faith in themselves and each other.

Eric and Jena started Civic Saturday in Seattle in the weeks after Donald Trump was first elected in 2016. Since that time, people in cities across the country have asked them to lead similar gatherings in their communities. Instead of looking to science to find a way to clone themselves, Eric and Jena looked to religion for a model that would meet this need. That's how they started Civic Seminary, a program that will teach people in the texts and rituals of American democracy and train them with the skills to lead their own Civic Saturdays.

What follows are three examples of how religion influences institution building for social change.

ISMAILI MUSLIMS AND THE AGA KHAN DEVELOPMENT NETWORK

One of the most remarkable things about the civic institutions established by religious communities is that they give adherents the opportunity to deepen into our own faith identity, feel more a part of our own religious history, embrace more fully our own community, *by serving the needs of people who fall outside of it.* This is one of the ways that institutions that are built by particular identity communities can nurture pluralism.

I am an Ismaili Muslim, part of a community of approximately fifteen million spread across some thirty countries. Ismailis, guided by our spiritual leader the Aga Khan, are institution builders extraordinaire.

As a response to the discrimination they experienced in colonial South Asia and Africa, Ismailis started a whole network of schools, hospitals, economic development organizations, and cultural initiatives for themselves. After colonialism ended, Ismailis, under the guidance of the Aga Khan, transformed those facilities into institutions that serve the broader public and organized them into the Aga Khan Development Network (AKDN).

The purpose of the AKDN is articulated in cosmic terms. It is the set of institutions that allows us to "realize the social conscience of Islam" by serving as a "bridge (between) the two realms of the faith, *din* and *dunya*, the spiritual and the material." In the words of Ismaili scholars describing the AKDN mandate: "Islam envisions a social order which is sustained by the expectation of each individual's morally just conduct towards others. The function of ethics is to foster self-realization through giving of one's self, for the common good, in response to God's benevolent majesty." [8]

The AKDN is probably the most widespread and sophisticated network of Muslim civic and charitable organizations in the world. It works in thirty nations in South and Central Asia and across the continent of Africa, running over a thousand separate projects and employing nearly one hundred thousand people. Two million people per year are educated through AKDN schools and universities; five million annually receive medical care through its health programs; eight million people in rural areas are made more food secure through AKDN initiatives; and ten million people have electricity because of AKDN infrastructure projects in developing nations. [9]

Aga Khan University in Karachi is probably the best university in the Muslim-majority world. It has a world-class medical program, with a particular strength in nursing, a profession that not only saves lives but also disproportionately employs women. Sensitivity to gender equity is a priority throughout the work of the AKDN, indeed in every quarter of the Ismaili community. Ismailis are perhaps the only Muslim community that have both female administrative leaders and female prayer leaders. My aunt, for example, was appointed by the Aga Khan as president of the world's largest Ismaili National Council (India), and my mother was appointed to be a worship leader at the *jamat khana* (house of worship) that my father helped to build in Naperville.

Gender is not the only dimension of identity that the AKDN pays attention to; pluralism in general is a core value. It goes beyond health and educational services being offered to people regardless of identity to mean an active "appreciation, tolerance, and openness towards other peoples' culture, social structures, values and beliefs." The value is most prominently displayed in the AKDN's cultural initiatives, which includes supporting the indigenous music, art, and architecture of a variety of diverse communities. One of my favorite AKDN initiatives is the support given to Yo-Yo Ma's Silk Road Project, which brought a diverse array of indigenous musical forms together in a single, magnificent sonic collaboration.

Like other global development networks, the AKDN receives funding from national governments and international agencies. But a substantial amount of the resources are contributed by the Aga Khan himself and the Ismaili community more broadly. The reason is simple: it is a requirement of Islam to help others, and the AKDN is the vehicle for Ismailis to manifest this Muslim commitment.

The Prophet Muhammad showed us that our everyday actions are suffused with spiritual significance. In his own life, he modeled the values of inclusiveness, inquiry, mercy, balance, care for the environment, and self-reliance. And so it is that teachers in AKDN schools, researchers in AKDN laboratories, doctors in AKDN hospitals, and artists in AKDN cultural programs seek, through their work, to embody this ethic.

David Brooks likes to say that social change happens when some people find a better way to live and other people start to copy them.[10]

That is precisely the theory of change the AKDN operates on. The various AKDN institutions are meant to model an ideal social order based on the ethics of Islam; the rest of the world is invited to follow.

ELLA BAKER AND SNCC

Here is what the sociologist of religion C. Eric Lincoln once wrote about the Black church in America: "Beyond its purely religious function, as critical as that function has been, the Black church in its historical role as lyceum, conservatory, forum, social service center, political academy, and financial institution, has been and is for Black America the mother of our culture, the champion of our Freedom, and the hallmark of our civilization."[11]

"Black church" does not refer only to brick-and-mortar buildings or to the people who wear a collar, like the Reverend Dr. Martin Luther King Jr., but rather to an entire galaxy of institutions and individuals, including many who are not readily identified with religion but were shaped by it just the same.

Take, for example, the great Ella Baker, perhaps the most influential woman in the civil rights movement. Ms. Baker did not wear a collar, was very much a grassroots ground-up organizer rather than a White House negotiator, and famously chafed against some of the more patrician male figures of the movement, notably King. According to Barbara Ransby's magisterial biography *Ella Baker and the Black Freedom Movement*, Baker approached the world this way *because* of her Christian formation, not in spite of it.[12]

Ella Baker's entire world was suffused with Christian influences. The historian Eric Anderson described the area in which Ella Baker was raised like this: "Protestant Christianity . . . permeated the district, touching people's lives more steadily than any other institution. . . . The very pervasiveness of religion obscured its boundaries with politics, society and work."[13]

As a little girl, Ms. Baker would ride in the horse-drawn buggy of her maternal grandfather, Reverend Mitchell Ross, a prominent Baptist minister in North Carolina, as he visited various churches.

He allowed her to sit in the deacon's chair behind the pulpit as he preached. Ella long remembered the combination of erudition and authority that emanated from her grandfather. For his part, Reverend Ross sensed something out of the ordinary in his favorite grandchild and often referred to Ella as "the grand lady."

And yet it wasn't so much the life of the congregation that shaped Ella (she was only required to go to church once a week, while many Black Baptists attended far more frequently), but rather the institutions that women formed within the broader Black Baptist Church galaxy. "I was young when I became active in things," Baker once said, "and I became active in things because my mother was very active in the field of religion." Women like Anna Ross Baker, Ella's mother, had built a state conference within the world of Black Southern Baptists. Out of this institution they ran several social welfare programs for African Americans ranging from an orphanage to grammar schools to scholarships for Black college students.

Women ran everything—the meetings, the budgets, the policy— and Ella watched, learned, and participated. The historian Evelyn Brooks Higginbotham describes it as a feminist theology in action that "within a female-centered context . . . accentuated the image of woman as saving force, rather than woman as victim. . . . They argued that women held the key to social transformation."[14]

When she was sixteen years old, Ella went to another set of institutions within the Black Southern Baptist galaxy: Shaw Academy and Shaw University. Shaw was not only the first historically Black institution of higher education in the South; it was also the first such institution to open its doors to women. The same Christian commitment to service that suffused Ella's childhood also pervaded Shaw. The curriculum emphasized the Christian inspiration for service to others. The leaders of the institution were generally returned missionaries or ministers. The motto of the school was "For Christ and humanity," and students were required to sing hymns with lyrics like, "Others, Lord, yes, others, and none of self for me. Help me to live for others that I might live like thee."

It made a deep impact on Ella Baker: "Where I went to school . . . you went there to give . . . the best of yourself to other people, rather than to extract from other people for your own benefit."[15]

Decades after she graduated from Shaw, Ella Baker watched in admiration as another group of young Black college students started putting their faith into action through the sit-in movement in cities like Greensboro and Nashville. Baker was growing frustrated with the sexism and overall aristocratic air of her work with Martin Luther King Jr.'s Southern Christian Leadership Conference, where, even though she held the title of executive director, she found herself making copies rather than making policy. The male leadership of SCLC wanted to talk to women about "how well they cooked, and how beautiful they looked." Ella Baker didn't want to talk about fashion; she wanted to talk about the importance of grassroots leadership for the civil rights movement and the need for direct action. Perhaps these brave students would be more amenable to that. She made a plan to gather them at her alma mater and see where their energy might lead.

And so began the Student Nonviolent Coordinating Committee.

It is common to think of SNCC as the secular sword to Martin Luther King Jr.'s shield of Christian love. But the truth, as Charles Marsh documents in his powerful book *The Beloved Community: How Faith Shapes Social Justice from the Civil Rights Movement to Today*, is that SNCC was very much founded as a Christian institution. Marsh writes: "SNCC's founding mothers and fathers were very often radical Christians, exuberantly faithful people motivated by diverse theological sources mixed in unusual, sometimes exotic, combinations according to the demands of the situation."[16]

At that conference at Shaw University—held appropriately over Easter weekend—the students, under the tutelage of Ella Baker, drafted a mission statement where they committed to building "a social order permeated by love and to the spirituality of nonviolence as it grows from the Christian tradition."

SNCC organizers described their strategies and tactics in scriptural terms. Sit-ins, according to Chuck McDew, were a reenactment of Jesus sitting with the Samaritan woman at the well and saying, "Please give me a glass of water." While the Samaritan woman noted the illicit nature of their being together, Jesus was simply making the point that there was enough water in the well for both of them and that fellowship between people of different identities was holy. By asking for a cup of coffee at a segregated lunch counter, SNCC activists were playing the Jesus role to the Samaritans of white America.

While SNCC would later take on a different flavor when Stokely Carmichael and the proponents of Black Power took charge, in its early years the organization manifested what Charles Marsh calls the "incarnational ethic" of the "enfleshed church." Rather than adopting the tailored suits favored by Martin Luther King Jr. and the clergy leaders of the SCLC, SNCC organizers wore denim overalls and work boots, a sartorial choice that helped them build trust with ordinary people in local communities throughout the South.

A field report from a young SNCC organizer named Charles Sherrod offers a glimpse into what the incarnational ethic of SNCC work actually looked like: "I have seen the church under the stars praying and singing in the ashes of burned down church buildings, in the winter shivering under a tent in the open country, in a home where people cried together without speech but with a common understanding. . . . I have seen men share their bread till the last was gone. I have seen a band of rugged brothers willing to risk death for each other if need be. I have seen the strength of fellowship among those who formally refuse the fellowship of the church."

The language is hauntingly beautiful, and very male. The truth is, we remember much of the civil rights movement through its very visible male leaders—giants like Roy Wilkins, Bayard Rustin, Martin Luther King Jr., and Ralph Abernathy. Virtually all of the main characters in the film *Selma* are men. SNCC in the early days undoubtedly had its fair share of influential male figures (John Lewis, Marion Barry, James Bevel, James Lawson, Bob Moses), but perhaps because of the powerful presence of Ella Baker, it was distinctive in the number of women who shaped the incarnational ethic of the organization. There was Diane Nash, one of the leaders of the Nashville sit-in movement, who reflected upon her time at the Shaw conference and the hope of SNCC in this way: "Our goal was to reconcile," to create a "community recovered or fulfilled . . . to redeem . . . to rehabilitate, to heal, to reconcile rather than gain power." SNCC for her was "applied religion."[17]

There was Fannie Lou Hamer, who spoke of SNCC and the civil rights movement as a welcome table, the kind that was often next to a rural Baptist church and that held the dishes the congregants contributed, allowing the whole community to enjoy a potluck feast. "Christ was a revolutionary person, out there where it's happening," she said. "That's what God is all about, and that's where I get my strength."[18]

There was Victoria Gray, a Black middle-class businesswoman who left her comfortable life to join the movement after being inspired by a church service in her hometown of Hattiesburg. She said these words as she made her choice: "Here am I, Lord, send me, I'll go." She regarded the civil rights movement as "a journey toward establishing the kingdom of God."[19]

BRYAN STEVENSON AND THE EQUAL JUSTICE INITIATIVE

I view Bryan Stevenson, founder and executive director of the Equal Justice Initiative, as the single most significant social change agent in America today. He works on the most divisive issues in our national life—the legacy of lynching, the racism that runs through the bloodstream of our criminal justice system, the disgrace of the death penalty—and somehow makes them feel uncontroversial, as if there are no enemies to defeat, only a widening camp of those climbing the mountain to the summit of justice.

He thinks in systems but communicates mostly through deeply affecting stories about individuals. He weaves beautifully complex meta-narratives and yet it never feels like he's talking over your head. He comes across as utterly humble and is still charismatic enough to be the central figure of a Hollywood movie, where he was played by the star Michael B. Jordan.

Robert Raben, one of my mentors, calls him the closest America gets to a living Mandela figure.

Bryan Stevenson began his work as a scrappy attorney taking on wrongful conviction and death penalty cases and has grown into a remarkable institution builder with a multifaceted vision. He has continued to fight, and win, cases related to capital punishment, including several at the Supreme Court. But he has recognized that fighting bad things after they happen cannot be a long-term strategy for achieving justice. So instead, he wants to change the way we understand the American story.

In Stevenson's view, it was only possible for the slavery-to-segregation-to-mass-incarceration evolution to occur because the United States never did the hard work of reckoning with its racist past. Germany has no Adolf Hitler statues; why does the United States have statues of people who terrorized Black people and committed treason against the nation like Robert E. Lee? Germany has markers in places where Jews were abducted and sent to concentration camps; shouldn't the United States do the same where the analogous took place on our soil? It is for this reason that Stevenson's Equal Justice Initiative, in addition to adding a spate of excellent lawyers to its staff, has built the National Memorial for Peace and Justice (also known as the National Lynching Memorial).[20]

If you listen to Bryan Stevenson for any length of time, either in the documentary about his work called *True Justice* or in interviews with journalists like Ezra Klein and Krista Tippett, you will hear resoundingly just how deeply his work is undergirded not just by his deep religious beliefs but also by the structures of faith institutions.[21]

Scripture from all traditions, he points out, is full of examples of people who sinned horribly and then, through a process of ritual cleansing, became redeemed. An archetypal story is Saul of Tarsus, who violently persecutes the early disciples of Jesus, and then, as a result of a religious vision, transforms his life, becoming Paul the Apostle, one of the most important figures in all of Christian history. It is this possibility for transformation, Stevenson says, that lies beneath the entire process of the Church. And it is this vision that Stevenson takes into his work with people who have been imprisoned. They are people who have committed crimes and who could, with the right process, be restored into the community. He tells Ezra Klein: "In my tradition, if you said 'If you've done any of these ten sins, then you can't come to our church, we won't accept you.' . . . You'd be mocked and ridiculed for not having enough faith. People would come after you for not having enough faith."[22]

This isn't just a belief system—it is an institutional structure. The way the Church works is by having a ritual process by which people can be forgiven for their sins and welcomed back as members of good standing in the community.

That is what Bryan Stevenson seeks to do with individuals who have committed crimes, to advance a justice system based not on punishment but redemption and restoration. And this is what he hopes to do for a nation that has committed genocidal crimes against both Indigenous people and African Americans.

The United States can only be liberated from our past if we fully reckon with it. It is a process of truth and reconciliation, but Stevenson cautions we can't move too quickly to reconciliation. The model, he emphasizes, is religion:

> In most traditions, we view confession, we view acknowledgement, we view the process of admitting to wrongdoing as an essential step towards redemption. In my faith tradition, you can't just walk into church and say, "I want heaven, I want all the good stuff, I want to be part of that number, but I don't want to talk about anything bad I've done." It doesn't work like that. You've got to repent. You've got to confess. And they tell you that the confession and the repentance isn't something you should fear, but it's something you should embrace because through that process comes a kind of awareness and awakening and even a cleansing that allows you to embrace and understand what redemption truly means, what recovery really means, what salvation really means.[23]

While Stevenson's Equal Justice Initiative isn't overtly a faith-based organization, it has organized what can only be called sacred rituals that facilitate the process he speaks to above. Amongst the most powerful is the ritual of handing people jars and sending them to sites where Black people were lynched. People take an instrument and dig up the dirt and put it in the jar. The jar is placed on a wall with the name of the lynched individual. In this way, says Stevenson, the lynched person is resurrected.

"There's sweat in that soil. The sweat of enslaved people. There are the tears of the people who suffered as they were being brutalized and lynched. There's the blood. But there's also hope in that soil."[24]

That is the power of religion and religious institutions. They guide and give hope, they cleanse and resurrect, they build and sustain.

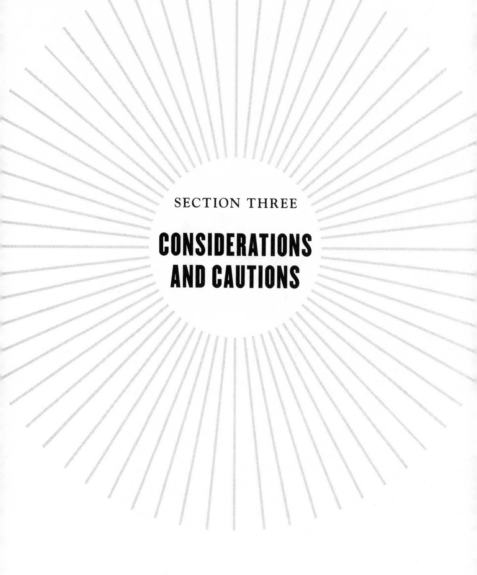

SECTION THREE

CONSIDERATIONS AND CAUTIONS

CHAPTER EIGHT

THE CHALLENGE
OF BEING IN CHARGE

"IT'S BETTER TO HAVE POWER THAN OUTRAGE." THAT'S what Larry Krasner said after pushing forward a proposal to end cash bail for minor offenses. Activists had long protested the cash bail system for essentially criminalizing poverty. If a kid from a rich family stole a pack of gum, he could get bailed out within a day. If a kid from a poor family did the same thing, he could possibly sit in jail for months, for want of a few hundred dollars.

Larry had been an activist for decades. He had spent thirty years as some combination of crusading public defender, civil rights attorney, and criminal defense lawyer. But this moment was different. He was no longer arguing against the district attorney in court or protesting a policy of the office from the outside. *He was the district attorney.* He led the office. He hired the staff. He made actual, consequential decisions about everything, from which crimes to prosecute to which police officers to bar from court because of egregious misconduct.

Speaking to a group of students, Larry described how he had "beat his head against the wall" of the criminal justice system from the outside for years and years, a process that resulted in the occasional win and a continuous headache. Now he was sitting in the chair of power, and he was making big changes. Amongst them: decriminalizing marijuana possession, promoting community programs over prison, and seeking shorter sentences. "When a movement has the chance to go on the inside, go with it," he told the students.[1]

The line by Frederick Douglass, "Power concedes nothing without a demand," is a mainstay in activist circles.[2] It makes a crucial point about the significance of struggle. *But what happens when you win? When you go from activist public defender to actual district attorney?*

Take the case of Rachael Rollins, a Black female progressive reformer who became the district attorney in Suffolk County, which includes both the city of Boston and the surrounding areas. She put it best when she told Krasner in a conversation: "I woke up September 5 [the day after she won election] and was like, 'Oh my God, this is amazing.' And then you realize what a big job this is." What happened if there was a rise in crime under her watch, she worried; would people blame it on her?[3]

The answer to that question is yes. You struggle against corrupt or oppressive power so that you might take it and wield it more effectively. When you win that struggle, when power concedes to your demand and you are the person in charge, you are making an implicit promise that people's lives will improve under your leadership. They will be safer and healthier, better educated and better paid, more comfortable and more fulfilled. Responsibility for improving people's lives is the other side of the coin of power. Crusading for a cause can feel intoxicating, and it's most certainly a release for justified anger. Bearing responsibility for other people's welfare can feel heavy. But why crusade for a cause, why struggle against power, unless you are prepared to carry that weight?

Ron Crutcher, a professional cellist and longtime college administrator has a story about being in charge and being responsible for other people's lives. As dean at the School of Music at the University of Texas, Ron had scheduled a meeting with a CEO of an oil company who was a well-known supporter of the arts. Ron's purpose was to raise money for a scholarship for violin study.

The first words out of the wealthy man's mouth after Ron shook his hand were, "I had no idea you were Black." It made Ron mad. He thought about leaving, but he knew that if he did someone else would suffer. He was there to raise a scholarship for a student who was relying on him. Ron had a serious responsibility and therefore little choice but to proceed with the meeting.

It turns out that the potential donor was frustrated that the world of classical music was so white, and he was excited that the dean he was sitting with was not just an accomplished musician and administrator but also a Black man. The donor was even more thrilled to learn that the scholarship for violin study that Ron was presenting would go to a woman of color. The man made the financial gift, the School of Music got its scholarship, and Ron's student went on to a coveted position in the Cleveland Orchestra.[4]

Offensive as the donor's first sentence surely had been, he actually had the same goals for diversity, equity, and inclusion that Ron had, he had just expressed himself poorly at the beginning of the meeting. Wasn't it better that Ron hadn't judged the man's character and intentions based on a single maladroit sentence?

Ron's story is a potent illustration of what it looks like to make social change when you are the one in charge. For me, it brings to mind Ibram X. Kendi's definition of anti-racism. Anti-racism in policy matters, Kendi writes, is not principally about the language, it's principally about the impact.[5] In that frame, I see Ron Crutcher's story as a case study in anti-racism. In his leadership position as dean, Ron felt as if he had both the responsibility and the power to make the school more diverse. In his story with this particular donor, Ron ignored the first offensive sentence, did the work to raise the scholarship, diversified the school by supporting a young artist of color, and built a friendship along the way.

"What would you have done?" Ron likes to ask the student he invites to dinner at the president's house at the University of Richmond.

During these dinners, Ron offers cautions and considerations with respect to making social change when you are the one in charge. Most certainly the donor's comment was racially insensitive, and Ron may well have been justified for declaring it so and leaving the meeting right then and there. But what would he have told his violin student who needed the scholarship to continue her studies? Shouldn't the person in charge consider the welfare of the people for whom he is responsible? And think about how the situation had turned out. The donor quickly expressed his enthusiasm for diversity and inclusion in classical music. It appears that his first words were simply poorly stated. Wasn't it wise to be cautious about jumping to conclusions?

This section is written in the spirit of those dinners that Ron Crutcher hosts at his house with student leaders, and which I've attended as a guest speaker at the University of Richmond. It's a collection of what I call considerations and cautions about how to achieve power in a way that builds people's trust and how to wield power in a way that improves people's lives. There's a reason that I am not calling these "dos and don'ts." I don't think of them as hard-and-fast rules, but more like the signs that warn you about a winding road up ahead, or ice on the bridge. If you seek to be in charge, it's good to have a sense of when you might need to slow down or when things are likely to get slippery.

CHAPTER NINE

ALIGN THE SUBSTANTIVE
AND THE SYMBOLIC

I N LATE JANUARY 2021, THE SAN FRANCISCO BOARD OF EDUCA-
tion gave its students and families new school names but no
schools.

While the pandemic continued to rage and low-wage workers continued to suffer, the school board spent its precious time on renaming
forty-four schools in its district. There was to be no more Abraham
Lincoln High School, no more Roosevelt Middle School, no more
Paul Revere Elementary. The statement from the school board said
that these individuals were responsible for subjugation, enslavement,
and genocide—or had been deemed as "otherwise significantly di-
minishing the opportunities of those amongst us to the right to life,
liberty, and the pursuit of happiness."[1]

Mayor London Breed opened her comments on the matter by
underscoring the importance of symbols, including school names.
It meant a lot to her personally to have graduated from an educational institution carrying the hallowed name of Rosa Parks. But, she
continued, "What I cannot understand is why the School Board is
advancing a plan to have all these schools renamed by April, when
there isn't a plan to have our kids back in the classroom by then. Our
students are suffering, and we should be talking about getting them

in classrooms, getting them mental health support, and getting them the resources they need in this challenging time."[2]

The students Mayor Breed was referring to were mostly poor and students of color. The national image of San Francisco tends to be its wealthy white liberals (think Nancy Pelosi), but the vast majority of those families send their children to expensive private schools. Nearly 90 percent of the San Francisco public school system is made up of kids of color whose parents do not have the financial privilege of choosing private education.

A main purpose of symbols like school names is to signal something about the substance. If you change the name on the school to better represent the student population, people assume that you have improved the classes and the teaching as well. If you haven't improved anything inside the school, or even opened the school for in-person instruction, then you have done the equivalent of giving people a hood ornament without a car.

In this case, the San Francisco Board of Education didn't even get the symbol right. The board justified the removal of Paul Revere's name from a school by claiming he had attacked a camp of Indigenous people. The incident in question was actually a raid on a British fort. A school board who aims to teach the public a lesson on history has an obligation to be accurate. If it gets basic facts wrong, it loses all credibility.

The liberal commentator Ezra Klein viewed the San Francisco school board story as a sign of a potentially large and grave problem. Democrats are in charge of virtually every level of meaningful government in California, but the social problems in the state continue to get worse, even as the flag of symbolic progressivism flies high. California is at the center of the climate change movement but still does not have proper mass transit, and of course the fumes from all those cars continue to spew carbon dioxide into the atmosphere. Neighborhoods in San Francisco that are dominated by "Black Lives Matter" and "No Human Being Is Illegal" signs are full of million-dollar homes and organized campaigns to maintain high housing prices, effectively excluding everyone but the 1 percent. In fact, once housing prices are factored in, California has amongst the worst poverty rates and highest income inequality of any state in the nation. "If progressivism cannot work here, why should the country believe it can work anywhere else?" Klein concludes.[3]

To return to the specific challenge of public schools, let's recognize that it was hard to figure out how to be in the classroom safely during the pandemic. But the science suggested that, with proper precautions, it was possible. Grocery stores figured it out, airports figured it out, post offices figured it out, Amazon figured it out—indeed, many schools figured it out. Across the country, most Catholic schools, which generally have far fewer resources than public schools, had in-person instruction. And public schools in areas governed by Republicans (which tended to be mostly white) did the same.

It was public schools that served predominantly poor and nonwhite kids, like those in my home city of Chicago, that did not open until late in the academic year. This, even though research convincingly showed that these students were the ones hurt most by closed schools, and despite eloquent speeches from urban public school leaders on the importance of improving education for these children in particular.[4]

Progressives have a historic opportunity to make their case. That case goes something like this: Hundreds of years of racism has led to gaping disparities, from income to health, and intractable problems, from street violence to police abuse, that are not going to be solved only by the market. It is going to take a massive effort of civic and governmental institutions to lift people out of poverty, to give ladders of opportunity to those who have been historically excluded, and to improve neighborhoods that have experienced chronic underinvestment. But if people's lives do not improve when progressives are in charge—for example, when school districts with progressive leadership are not open while school districts with conservative leadership are—progressive commitments run the risk of being viewed as not just ineffective but also downright fraudulent.

Here is a well-known model of social change, drawn from the Movement Action Plan. According to this model, social movements work through three main objectives:

1. Prove there is a problem.
2. Prove that the existing approaches and institutions meant to solve this problem are not working.
3. Prove that the movement's alternatives work better.[5]

We live at a time when more and more people see the problem. More and more people are unsatisfied with the existing approaches. More and more people are willing to take a chance on a different approach, different leaders, different institutions.

What do you think happens if you point out all the ways the current education system is unfair, tell them to trust you to make the schools better, and then spend your energy on changing the names of school buildings that the kids who most need them can't go to? What do you think happens if people give you their trust and you give them back a new school name without an actual school?

If you point fingers at what others are doing wrong, people will turn to you and ask if you can put it right. If you promise them you can, people expect you to keep your promise. Generally speaking, people will not accept a hood ornament in place of a car, especially when they desperately need to travel to a destination.

The point is not to be less progressive but rather to be more substantive. The point is not to diminish the power of symbols; instead, it is to align the symbolic and the substantive.

CHAPTER TEN

BE GUIDED BY A VISION FOR, NOT AN ANGER AGAINST

ON A SUMMER NIGHT IN 1961, JAMES BALDWIN PRESENTED himself on the doorstep of the Honorable Elijah Muhammad. He had come for dinner because he heard in the language of Elijah Muhammad someone willing, at that time, to do the rarest of things: talk plainly in public about the pain and fury that Black people had suffered at the hands of white racism. The story of this dinner and Baldwin's reflections on it make up the bulk of his much-celebrated *The Fire Next Time*.

Over the course of the evening, Baldwin found himself growing increasingly uncomfortable, even alarmed. The men and women were separated in the Nation of Islam, and the women were very clearly subservient. Everything Elijah Muhammad said was met with immediate and total affirmation from the group, in a rhythmic formulaic manner befitting a cult, not a community. Did they really think they could create an entirely separate Black nation and economy? If Elijah Muhammad said so, they did. Did Elijah Muhammad really think that white people could only ever be evil and that their main purpose was to find ever more creative ways to poison Black people? Baldwin better not share that he was on his way to the North Side of the city to have a drink with a white friend later that night.

Ultimately, Baldwin comes to the realization that while he understands Elijah Muhammad's anger, he does not want to live in Elijah

Muhammad's world. "As I sat at Elijah's table and watched the baby, the women, and the men, and we talked about God's—or Allah's—vengeance, I wondered, when that vengeance is achieved, *What will happen to all that beauty then?*"[1]

He is referring to the Black people he grew up with in Harlem and coming to the realization that, although Elijah's anger is meant to save them, it won't because it can't. Anger doesn't construct, it only destroys. Burns everything. Including those who breathe the fire—however justified and righteous—in the first place.

Let me use an illustration from *Game of Thrones*. In the early seasons of the series, we watch Daenerys Targaryen grow into her leadership and set her sights on the Iron Throne. She is righteous and idealistic, dedicating herself to the cause of oppressed people across the Seven Kingdoms. She travels to city after city with her dragons at her side, inspiring crowds with her speeches about equality and freedom, and directing her dragons to burn down the structures of enslavement.

Along the way, she learns that if you burn a structure down, people expect you to build something better in its place. Dragon fire proves to be a powerful weapon against oppression, but a hazard to good governance. Dragons cannot tell the difference between a brutal slave master and an innocent farmer. They just scorch everything in sight.

Season after season, we see Daenerys struggle with governing and become more and more wedded to her dragons. She increasingly sees the world through their eyes. Watching her become angrier and angrier, I couldn't help but think about a twist on an old adage: "If all you have is the anger of dragon fire, the whole world looks like a structure to burn."

The final episodes of the series bring this theme to its logical conclusion. When the bells ring at King's Landing, announcing the surrender of the city, no look of relief or celebration crosses Daenerys Targaryen's face. She does not think to herself that the day she has waited for these long and brutal years has finally arrived and that her golden reign of peace and justice might begin. She has had too much experience burning things down and too little building them up. She rides her dragon high into the sky, her whole body a clenched fist of oppositional fury even at the hour of her victory, and rains down a raging fire, murdering the very people she had promised to save.

And she is not finished yet. In her first formal speech as queen of the Seven Kingdoms, she promises more death, more destruction, more burning down of structures. This madness, even though she now sits upon the Iron Throne and has all the power she needs to build a better world.

The Daenerys Targaryen spirit lives in history as much as it does in fiction. The French Revolution began with the cry of liberty, equality, and fraternity and then gave way to five years of the Reign of Terror and, finally, a new dictator, Napoleon. Such has been the fate of more than one movement that began with high ideals. Too many activists, in their zeal to overthrow the Shah, wound up installing the Ayatollah. Some of them became the Ayatollah.

So what is to be done with righteous anger? Baldwin transforms his into working for the possibility of America.

"I am not a ward of America," he writes. "I am one of the first Americans to arrive on these shores." That gives him both greater privileges, and also, in his estimation, greater responsibilities. He writes, "Everything now, we must assume, is in our hands; we have no right to assume otherwise." And what should we do with that responsibility? Here is Baldwin's answer: come together across racial lines to "achieve our country" and, by doing this, "change the history of the world."[2]

CHAPTER ELEVEN

EMBRACE DIVERSITY, INCLUDING THE DIFFERENCES YOU DON'T LIKE

M Y FRIEND ASMA UDDIN IS AN AMERICAN MUSLIM CIVIL rights attorney who both tries cases about, and writes books on, religious freedom. She likes to begin her public talks by presenting summaries of a set of diverse cases: a Muslim prisoner case, a case involving Native Americans' access to sacred eagle feathers, a case challenging Oklahoma's anti-sharia law, the fight by the Knights of Columbus to keep a statue of Jesus on federally owned but privately leased land, and the infamous *Hobby Lobby* case, where a company privately owned by conservative Christians sued the Obama administration over its requirement that businesses include health insurance coverage for contraception as part of the Affordable Care Act.

Asma's audiences evince what has become the standard American polarization over these issues. Liberals find themselves siding with the minority groups, such as the Muslim prisoner and the Native Americans seeking access to eagle feathers. Conservatives align themselves with the Knights of Columbus and Hobby Lobby.

Asma surprises everyone when she announces that she is a supporter of all the groups, even the ones whose views she disagrees with and whose identities she doesn't especially like. The same principle of religious freedom, as articulated in the First Amendment and also in the Religious Freedom and Restoration Act of 1993, applies to each party—indeed to all of us.

In her book *The Politics of Vulnerability*, Asma tells the story of going on Al Jazeera America to explain why she had argued the *Hobby Lobby* case in the Supreme Court, on the side of the conservative Christians who sued the Obama administration. She is fully aware that, as she puts it, "Brown-skinned religious minorities are traits of the liberal mega-identity, and religious cases brought by white conservative Christians indisputably belong to the conservative mega-identity."[1] She enjoyed the double take that the image of her defending Hobby Lobby on television must have caused people across the political spectrum. "A nonwhite, American Muslim woman defending Hobby Lobby on a Qatari-owned television network? That's a stark disruption of our tribal mega-identities."

But Asma's purpose is not to cause disruption; rather, it's to uphold a set of key principles. The ability to practice faith freely, without undue interference by the government as guaranteed by United States law and belonging equally to all, is one such principle. Stanford law professor and former appellate judge Michael McConnell writes about why the Supreme Court has sided with a host of diverse religious groups, ranging from minority faiths to the Christian majority. Asma quotes him approvingly: "[these decisions] can be seen not as advancing the left or the right, but instead as protecting pluralism—the right of individuals and institutions to be different, to teach different doctrines, to dissent from dominant cultural norms and to practice what they preach."[2]

The second principle she cites is from Islam, the faith we share, that we both believe calls on us to embrace diversity, including the differences we don't like. She quotes the famous verse from the Qur'an in which God says, "O mankind, indeed We have created you from male and female and made you peoples and tribes that you may come to know one another."[3] Put simply, the way Asma interprets Islam is that her Muslim identity requires her to ensure the thriving of everybody else's identity in a diverse society.

The final principle she discusses is the principle of friendship, whose sacredness the Qur'an verse above suggests in the phrase "come to know one another." We live at a time where it seems normal to look for the worst in people with identities we dislike, to wish harm on those with whom we disagree, sometimes even to cause that harm. But how do you have a diverse democracy when you are constantly looking to demonize your fellow citizens? Asma wants something different. She actively seeks to cultivate friendships with people from different identities, most recently by launching a set of conversations with Evangelical Christian partners. Here is how she describes the role, and experience, of the bridge builder: "For those of us like me, who prefer to stand in the middle, to ask questions, be curious, and point out the reasonable elements of each side in an attempt to truly effect change, the experience can be frightening."[4]

Still, she keeps at it. Speaking to progressive groups about the importance of standing up for the freedom of Christian conservatives in court. Speaking to Christian conservatives about the importance of welcoming Muslims and other religious, racial, and ethnic minorities as equal citizens in American civic and political life.

This is where Asma's work as a lawyer and a writer and Interfaith America's work on college campuses have the most overlap. I increasingly encounter student groups on campus who have developed a policy of not engaging with organizations with which they disagree. If they don't like the other group's stance on, say, the conflict in the Middle East, then they won't participate in college events like panel discussions or conferences.

Here is what I ask the students in these groups: Imagine you are a heart surgeon and you are scheduled to be part of a team of surgeons that is performing a life-saving operation. Let's say you discover that one of the other surgeons or a nurse supporting the surgery disagrees with you on a political issue dear to your heart. Maybe that person voted differently in the last election and advertises it with a bumper sticker on her car. Do you refuse to do the heart surgery?

To date, not a single person has said they would walk out of the operating room.

I continue along the same path: what about a PTA? Or a volunteer fire department? Most students agree that it is important to stay involved in those activities working alongside people you disagree with because the activity is a benefit to the society.

Civic life in general, including panel discussions between student groups with different views, benefits all of us. To be a citizen of a diverse democracy means being able to disagree on some fundamental things while working together on other fundamental things.

When I shared this story with Asma, she quoted from the Qur'an: "Repel evil with good, and your enemy will become like an intimate friend."[5]

CHAPTER TWELVE

EMBRACE THE MULTIPLE
LANGUAGES OF SOCIAL CHANGE

I N 1984, PAUL SIMON FOUND HIMSELF DOWN IN THE DUMPS. HIS
marriage had soured, his career had taken a turn for the worse,
he needed something to pick him up. Right about that time, a friend
handed him a cassette with the peculiar title *Gumboots: Accordion
Jive Hits, Volume II.* The music was joyful and infectious. Simon could
not stop listening to it.[1]

Finally, he resolved to find the band behind his favorite songs
on the tape and, if at all possible, play music with them. That band
turned out to be a vocal group in South Africa called Ladysmith
Black Mambazo. Simon reached out and made contact, received a
warm response, and made arrangements to visit.

But there was one big problem: the United Nations had declared a
cultural boycott of South Africa to protest the brutality of the apartheid regime. The strategy of the activists who had led the campaign
was to put pressure on the government by choking off any kind of
exchange with the outside world.

Paul Simon had never been a political artist. He was not interested in making a statement; he was interested in making music. The
songs on that tape had lifted him out of a dark place. He wanted to
meet the musicians who made the songs, and if possible, he wanted to
work with them to put more music like that into the world. In order
to do that, he had to go where the beautiful sounds were, and they

happened to be coming from South Africa. He wasn't interested in self-promotion or money. Indeed, he had turned down an opportunity to earn huge fees by playing at the whites-only resort of Sun City.

Still, an array of activists in South Africa mobilized in opposition to Simon's visit, claiming that any violation of the boycott, even one done in the name of creating beauty, should be protested.

Many South African musicians viewed matters differently. The band Ladysmith Black Mambazo had received Paul Simon's overtures enthusiastically and invited him to come play with them. They were eager for the exchange and collaboration.

Others believed that this was not only benefiting the cause of beautiful music but also the cause of South African freedom. Musician and longtime American civil rights activist Harry Belafonte helped arrange the trip. While he had mixed feelings and hoped Simon would use the opportunity to speak with the activists, Belafonte generally believed that more exposure of South African culture to the world was better for freedom than less exposure.

Prominent South African musical icons like Hugh Masekela and Miriam Makeba expressed no mixed feelings at all, just strong support. They loved the idea that Paul Simon was making music in their country and pushed for him to tour with African musicians once *Graceland* was finished. They credited the album, the tours, and the accompanying exposure with dramatically increasing global interest in the struggle against apartheid.

None of this was Paul Simon's primary purpose in going to South Africa. He wasn't using music as a proxy for politics; he was playing music for its own sake. And he was proud of that conviction. "I'm with the musicians," he told a crowd of journalists who pressed him on why he had the temerity to violate the cultural boycott. "The artists always get screwed. The guys with the guns . . . on either the left or the right . . . say 'This is important,' and the guys with guitars don't have a chance."[2]

But, as Simon makes clear in a conversation with Dali Tambo, one of the activists who most vehemently opposed his visit to South Africa, the people with the guitars actually do make a big difference in the world. But they do so not by following the dictates of politicians or soldiers or even activists. Rather, they make a difference by doing what they do best: play music and make art. The language of beauty is an entirely different language from the language of politics; it operates by a totally different logic and proceeds by a different set of terms. It should not be viewed as the cart to the horse of someone else's political program. In Simon's view, we suffer politics so that we can create art and form friendships.[3]

Joseph Shabalala's view on the situation also centered on the art and the friendships. Shabalala was the founder of Ladysmith Black Mambazo, and Paul Simon was the first white man he ever hugged. (Immediately after he did it, Shabalala thought he might be put in jail.) He drew this broader lesson from his time making music with Paul Simon: "People, despite their color and their creed and where they come from, can work together. That's what *Graceland* meant to me."[4] The album, in other words, was many things—beautiful music, wind in the sails of the struggle against apartheid, and a premonition of what a multiracial South Africa might look like and sound like.

Imagine if those activists trying to keep Paul Simon out of South Africa were successful. Imagine if *Graceland* had not been made— if Paul Simon had succumbed to the pressure and not visited, not met and played music with Joseph Shabalala and Ladysmith Black Mambazo. If all those tours with African musicians had never happened. You'd have to erase the sustained global interest in the struggle against apartheid that followed. You'd have to delete the most iconic global image of the possibility of multiracial South Africa during the apartheid era. You'd have to imagine that one of the most remarkable albums in rock music history never got made.

I don't think that would have been a better world.

The point here is not that boycotts are bad or that political activists are wrong. Boycotts have changed the world, and activists are often prescient. The point is simply that uncompromising methods are not the *only* strategy for social change. There are moments for stridency and moments for melody.

Let us be clear: there would have been no struggle against apartheid to join had South African activists not built, over decades and at great sacrifice, a mighty movement. They are heroes who won the war, helped along by Paul Simon and Ladysmith Black Mambazo at the battle of *Graceland*.

CHAPTER THIRTEEN

BE CAREFUL TURNING IDENTITY CATEGORIES INTO IDEOLOGICAL CATEGORIES

I T DIDN'T GO OVER WELL WITH ANYONE WHEN JOE BIDEN SAID, during the 2020 presidential campaign, that Black people who supported Donald Trump "ain't Black."

The response from Black Republicans was predictable. Tim Scott of South Carolina, the only African American member of that party in the Senate, pointed out that 1.3 million Black people had voted Republican in the presidential race of 2016, and they didn't like having someone erase their Blackness on account of their political views.[1]

What was perhaps more surprising was the response from some Black progressives. "This is the natural consequence of the reductive view of race & politics pushed by the 'identity is destiny' crowd," wrote Briahna Joy Gray, former campaign secretary to Bernie Sanders.

I have been on both sides of the "identity is destiny" equation, with some particularly vivid memories from my college years. I remember when a professor announced that he had set up an online chat for class discussion (this was in the early days of the internet, when such arrangements were rare) because he claimed that Asian American students were more likely to offer their thoughts through a computer screen than in class. At this point he gave me a knowing look, as if to say, *I see you're Asian; you should know I did this for you.*

I recall being livid. I far preferred in-person discussion to anything online (I still do), and I was furious that he would make an assumption about me based on my skin color, even if that assumption was about something relatively minor.

My distaste at having someone else treat my identity deterministically on something small did not stop me from doing the same to others about things that were far more significant.

In my second year of college, I served as president of my residence hall, and the vice president serving alongside me, Doug, was Black. I was at the height of my identity politics fervor, and I wanted Doug to view race the way I did. I called myself oppressed; I wanted Doug to do the same. I was vocally opposed to the university's mascot, the racist Chief Illiniwek, and I wanted our whole executive committee to take a public stand on the topic. I thought Doug's voice, as a Black student, would be especially powerful. I pestered him constantly. "Why don't you speak out?" I asked.

Doug was not interested in speaking out on the Chief or calling himself oppressed. He wanted to use his year as vice president to convince the housing department at the University of Illinois to install benches outside of our residence hall. "It'll give people a comfortable place to sit when they're hanging out," he reasoned.

That's where Doug was going to focus his energies? I was flabbergasted. "Why do something small and concrete when we could do something large and symbolic?" I asked him. My thinking went something like this: If Doug would only become his true self, the radical self that I was convinced was inside every person of color, the revolution might start in our residence hall.

For the first few weeks Doug shrugged off my hounding. But finally, it simply got to be too much: "Why do you think you have a right to tell me what my identity is? I am the one who decides who I am and what my views are, not you."

An excellent point. Telling someone else who they are—or more accurately, who you want them to be—is the height of presumptuousness. Just consider the wide range of assumptions being made. You are assuming, based on race or gender, what a person's experiences are, how they rank those experiences, and how they interpret them. As I wrote earlier, people are not like Russian nesting dolls. You cannot and should not assume that the inner dolls of political worldview, psychological disposition, or aesthetic preferences somehow look exactly like you want them to based on knowing the skin color of the outer doll.

For the life of me, I cannot explain why, after disliking when someone made assumptions about my preferences based on my skin color, I so brazenly turned around and did the same to others.

Beyond violating individual agency, assuming that someone's group identity determines their political worldview threatens the diversity within a community. The simple fact is that there are Black Republicans and Black Democrats, Black country singers and Black rappers, Black police officers and Black protestors who want to abolish the police. In Spike Lee's film *BlacKkKlansman*, both Ron Stallworth and his girlfriend are involved in Black empowerment. Patrice is the president of the Black Student Union that invites the radical Kwame Ture to give a fiery speech about revolution. Ron is a police officer, sworn to protect order. Patrice loves Ron but is highly skeptical about whether a Black person can be for the advancement of Black people and also be a cop. Ron believes it's possible, because he's doing it.[2]

While I'm proud to be a Democrat, I don't think Joe Biden gets to say who is and who is not Black based on political ideology.

CHAPTER FOURTEEN

SEEK SOLUTIONS,
THEN SEEK SCALE

M UHAMMAD YUNUS CAME TO THE UNITED STATES IN THE
1960s as a graduate student in economics and ultimately
earned his PhD from Vanderbilt. He returned to Bangladesh in the
early 1970s and took up the position of chair of the economics department at the University of Chittagong in the midst of a terrible fam-
ine. He watched as people came from the villages of Bangladesh into
the cities to starve to death. They chanted no slogans, they made no
demands, they simply lay down on the sidewalks—old people looking
like children, and children like old people—and waited for the last
moments of life to pass into the first moments of death.

Yunus began to dread his own economics lectures. After all, what
good were complex theories about making the flow of resources more
efficient when he was watching the most basic resource, food, miss its
most important target, hunger?

Yunus decided that he simply could not accept this reality. Why
was the most unconscionable thing imaginable simply an accepted
fact of life? How could he go to his fancy office in the midst of people
dying from hunger?

One of the poor people he interviewed was a woman named Sufiya, twenty-one years old with three beautiful, hungry children. Every day, Sufiya paid an unscrupulous middleman twenty-two cents
for raw bamboo, which she wove into elegant stools, much desired by

wealthy people in Bangladesh. She would sell a single bamboo stool back to the middleman for twenty-four cents. Her profit of two cents per day was just about enough to feed her family and keep a rickety roof over her head.

If Sufiya could sell the bamboo stools herself, her profit would have quadrupled. That additional money would have allowed her to buy more nutritious food, invest in better shelter, perhaps even have her children educated. Sufiya was suffering for the absence of twenty-two cents—the cost of purchasing her own bamboo. She didn't have that most basic of economic tools—access to capital.

Yunus did a survey of the village and discovered forty-two people in the same situation as Sufiya. Forty-two people trapped in a vicious, never-ending cycle of poverty for the lack of two dimes and two pennies per day.

He fished in his pocket, and for the now-famous sum of $27, he lifted forty-two people out of poverty.

Something wouldn't let Yunus sleep that night. He thought of all the villages like Jobra across Bangladesh, across South Asia, across the whole developing world. He thought of all the villagers like Sufiya—talented, hard-working people, suffering for the lack of small amounts of capital. And he had an idea.

What if there was a bank that treated poor people like resources worthy of financial investments, like producers with the capacity to create value? What if people like Sufiya in villages all over the world had access to capital?

Yunus didn't picket outside of banks telling them to solve the problem. He didn't spend all his time bemoaning to friends about the problem. He created a solution himself, in the form of an institution called the Grameen Bank that made microloans to collectives of women (mostly) so that they could grow their businesses and improve their lives. And then he scaled it, raising over $100 million in the 1980s and early 1990s, and working all over the world, shifting the narrative about the potential of poor people in the process.[1]

CHAPTER FIFTEEN

WELCOME ALL ALLIES

THERE HAVE BEEN SEVERAL SUPREME COURT JUSTICES WHO have shifted the course of history and a handful that have been worthy of biographies. But it is safe to say that there is only one who inspired a cottage industry in Halloween costumes for little girls and tattoos for slightly older ones. That person is Justice Ruth Bader Ginsburg.

Given her legendary status, it might surprise you to learn that the Supreme Court appointment for Ruth Bader Ginsburg almost did not happen. It wasn't retrograde men who tried to stop this remarkable female attorney who all but invented the field of gender discrimination law from a seat on the nation's highest court—it was actually progressive women.

Toward the end of her career, Ginsburg became known for her forceful dissents. But as Jill Lepore highlights, this was actually the exception rather than the rule. The defining quality of Ginsburg's legal work, both as an attorney and as a judge, was modesty and incrementalism. She was judicious to a fault, even claiming at one point that *Roe v. Wade* was the right decision at the wrong time. She would have preferred abortion rights laws to have made their way through state legislatures rather than be preempted by a Supreme Court decision.[1]

The remark, made during a talk at New York University School of Law, prompted some activist women's groups to communicate to

President Bill Clinton that they would prefer someone who was more forthrightly in support of their agenda *in all its particulars.*

What a tragedy it would have been if they had gotten their way. Ruth Bader Ginsburg was not just an ally but also a ringleader. She was a woman with a singular mind, a long-term vision, and remarkable courage. She just did her work differently than other activists.

"Fight for the things that you care about, but do it in a way that will lead others to join you," Ruth Bader Ginsburg once remarked.[2] That's another way of saying, welcome all allies and look to convert others, whatever their preferred style or symbolism. Even on matters of substance, we should be enlarging the tent and opening the doors wide. Purity tests are the enemy of broad-based movements. On this we should take a lesson from how Ronald Reagan built the Republican Party of the late twentieth century. Reagan was famous for telling fellow conservatives that the person who agrees with you on 80 percent of things is not best described as a 20 percent traitor.

CHAPTER SIXTEEN

PERSUADE YOUR OPPONENTS

O N SEPTEMBER 16, 2017, HAWK NEWSOME TRAVELED FROM
New York City to Washington, DC, to protest against a pro-
Trump event called the Mother of All Rallies.

Hawk was part of Black Lives Matter New York. He had come
to the DC protest because he was tired of the open racism coursing
through American public discourse. Hawk had most recently been on
the front lines in Charlottesville, and he was not going to back down
from a confrontation.

The pro-Trumpers looked ready to give him one, belligerently
chanting, "USA, USA," in his face.

But then something remarkable happened. The organizer of the
Mother of All Rallies, Tommy Hodges, invited Hawk on stage. He
said something about everybody having a right to their message and
gave Hawk two minutes on stage to deliver his.

Hawk used his two minutes well. He said he wasn't anti-cop, just
anti–bad cop. And just as bad plumbers should be fired, so should
bad cops. In this way, he was employing a research-backed approach
that encourages progressives to state their policy positions within
frames that conservatives resonate with, like firing people who do
a bad job.[1]

When an audience member shouted, "All lives matter," Hawk
agreed, and then responded that the reason for the Black Lives Matter movement is because there needs to be an extra emphasis on the

lives of Black people because they are frequently and often violently rolled over by the institutions of the state.

The pro-Trump crowd started cheering. When Hawk came off the stage, one of the pro-Trumpers asked if they could take a picture with his kid. Another treated a cut on his finger, a wound Hawk had suffered while opening a box with a knife earlier that day.[2]

This, it seems to me, is what effective activism looks like: a positive engagement of the people with whom you disagree.

It's also the only way to have a healthy diverse democracy.

By all means, preach to your choir, help them learn the song, teach them to sing it loud. But at some point you're going to have to talk to people with whom you disagree. Instead of further cementing the current Us vs. Them, wouldn't it be nice to create a wider sense of "Us"? Instead of constantly saying, "Here is my bright line that you can't cross," wouldn't it be great to say, "Here is my wide circle that you can join—it's a place where we will all thrive"?

CHAPTER SEVENTEEN

CONSIDER CONSTRUCTIVE ENGAGEMENT BEFORE YOU CANCEL

H ONESTLY, I THOUGHT IT WAS AN ACT THAT POTENTIALLY justified getting cancelled. Ralph Northam, the Democratic governor of the Commonwealth of Virginia, had apparently worn blackface while he was a medical student. Medical students are supposed to do no harm, right? And it was the 1980s, not the 1890s. I don't think it's too much to ask our political leaders to show a modicum of human decency and general sensitivity throughout adulthood.

The activist Quentin James, leader of the progressive Collective PAC, told *Vox News*, "People of color around him would be advising him to resign."[1]

Actually, it was not just people of color. Virginia's two white senators released a joint statement calling on Northam to step down. So did virtually every national Democratic leader. Joe Biden, who was at that time still running in the Democratic presidential primary, said that Northam had "lost all moral authority and should resign immediately."[2]

Northam did not resign. Nor did he take the Roy Cohn/Donald Trump path of denial, defiance, and vows of revenge against opponents. Instead, Northam admitted error, sought forgiveness, and asked the people who seemed most hurt and angry to help him change.

Even as the calls to cancel grew louder, a group of veteran Black leaders accepted Northam's invitation to work with him. At a widely covered news conference, they asked the Black community, and the broader public, to give him another chance. Bernice Travers, a Black activist in Richmond, was part of the group. She admitted that younger Black activists were at first frustrated with her and the other leaders who stood by Northam, but she advised them that sometimes the carrot can work better than the stick. When they hurled accusations that she was selling out and being used, she responded, "We didn't see ourselves as being used. We saw ourselves as looking at an opportunity to get this man to create some laws and programs that can move Black people forward."[3]

And move the Black community forward is precisely what happened. At the end of his tenure as governor, the *New York Times* called Northam the most progressive leader in the history of Virginia, especially on matters of racial justice. Under Northam's leadership, Virginia abolished the death penalty (it was the first state in the South to do so), allocated over $300 million to Virginia's network of Black colleges, and created a cabinet-level position in diversity, equity, and inclusion. Northam took down Confederate statues, replaced a state holiday honoring Confederate generals with one intended to expand voting access, and placed over twenty-five markers commemorating Black history across the state.[4]

Black leaders were part of the process every step of the way, including during the early days when the calls to cancel were loudest. Virtually all the Black staff who served in the Northam administration chose to stay by the governor's side instead of resigning in a show of protest. During the same period of intense pressure, the Virginia Legislative Black Caucus was preparing to work with the governor on policy goals. Even the Black activist community shifted its focus from the symbolic struggle of cancelling the governor to the substance process of working with him to build something better.

For his part, Governor Northam freely admitted that he had blinders on when it came to race for most of his life. He confessed not only to wearing blackface as a student but also to knowing little about the challenges facing Black people, from deep poverty to the racist use of capital punishment. The scandal was the impetus for change. Racial equity became one of Northam's top priorities. He devoured a whole literature of racial justice books. He started reaching out to Black leaders and opening with the question, "What can I do for you?"

One of the people he spoke with was the Black mayor of Danville, Virginia, Alonzo Jones. Jones was proud of both the changes that were ultimately made and the process that Northam and Black Virginians traveled together. The story of the partnership, he told the *New York Times*, "[was] a powerful antidote to a society struggling with cancel culture and wokeness. Instead of derision, Mr. Northam and the Black leaders who supported him showed the power of redemption, humility and growth."[5]

Mayor Jones continued: "Black people have always had to believe in forgiveness, and understanding. And I know a lot of times people want to argue that it hasn't gotten us anywhere, but I tend to disagree."

The results, measured in both substantive change and beautiful friendships, speak for themselves.

CHAPTER EIGHTEEN

STAND ON THE BALCONY
AND THINK OF A HEDGEHOG

"THE BALCONY" IS A METAPHOR MADE FAMOUS BY THE leadership scholar Ronald Heifetz. He says that the problem with most institutions is that the leaders are constantly on the dance floor, furiously moving their bodies to the music along with their staff and volunteers. It's important to be in the mix in the right ways, but what leaders really need to do is get up on the balcony.[1] That's the only way to see the patterns on the floor, get a sense of whether the music should be louder or softer, faster or slower. The more attuned you are to the patterns from the balcony perspective, the more you get a sense of what bigger improvements can be made to the space.

It was opportunities to "get on the balcony"—namely, retreats at the Alex Haley Farm in rural Tennessee—that changed things for Geoffrey Canada. He had been running an organization called the Rheedlen Centers for Children and Families, whose purpose was to help kids in Harlem escape crime and do better in school. The problem was that Rheedlen was stuck in the narrative of helping some kids beat the odds. Middle-class white kids in the suburbs of Kansas City could just be average and expect to live a decent life—graduate from college, own a home, live in a safe neighborhood, etc. Why did poor Black kids in Harlem have to be both exceptionally good and exceptionally lucky to achieve even half of that?

Moreover, why did organizations like Rheedlen have waiting lists for their programs? Shouldn't everyone who wanted to participate in enrichment programs have the opportunity? Actually, wasn't it the case that the kids in Harlem who *didn't* sign up for Rheedlen's programs needed them more? After all, seven-year-olds don't enroll themselves in tutoring; their parents do. And if you were a seven-year-old in Harlem whose parents didn't enroll you, you were probably further behind on reading than the seven-year-olds whose parents did sign them up.

Those retreats at the Alex Haley Farm helped Geoffrey Canada realize that it was time to flip the script. Instead of talking about helping a few kids beat the odds in Harlem, he started to talk about changing the odds. Instead of a set of ad hoc light-touch enrichments, his organization would create a web of cradle-to-college programs, analogous to the kinds of activities you would find in most middle-class neighborhoods, and drop that entire web over several dozen blocks in Harlem. Also, the organization would no longer be known as the Rheedlen Centers. It would now be the Harlem Children's Zone. And you wouldn't have to sign up for most of the programs; HCZ's organizers would come looking for you.

In *Good to Great*, the business guru Jim Collins urges leaders to identify the single big idea that their institution is about. He calls it the hedgehog concept (after the philosopher Isaiah Berlin's essay "The Hedgehog and the Fox") and cautions leaders to be patient before fully settling on it. It's not the kind of thing that emerges from a single whiteboard session with your executive team, but rather from a thousand experiments plus a million conversations mixed with the right flashes of insight.[2] For Geoffrey Canada, the moment came when he was staring at a waiting list for one of the Rheedlen Centers' programs. Why, after dealing with all of the challenges of living in that pocket of Harlem, did parents who wanted better opportunities for their children *have to deal with waiting lists for programs other people took as birthright?*

Geoffrey Canada had stood on the balcony and seen his hedgehog. The Harlem Children's Zone was going to take the necessary steps to get poor Black kids in Harlem achieving at the same levels as middle-class white kids in the suburbs of Kansas City. They were going to be attentive to the knowledge base they were acquiring along the way, and then they were going to show similar communities how to do the same.

The writer Paul Tough points out that none of the individual programs HCZ runs "are particularly revolutionary. It is only when they are considered together, as a network, that they seem so new."[3] That ability to implement a vision through a coordinated network of programs—that can only be accomplished by an institution.

CHAPTER NINETEEN

APPRECIATE THE HISTORY OF YOUR MOVEMENT, THEN EXTEND IT

A S I WROTE EARLIER, THE HEDGEHOG CONCEPT OF THE organization Interfaith America is to create the nation Interfaith America. We define it as a nation that welcomes its religious diversity from atheism to Zoroastrianism, nurtures positive relationships between those different groups, and engages them in common action for the common good. We believe Interfaith America should replace our current understanding of America as a Judeo-Christian nation. The Judeo-Christian narrative was incomplete and imperfect, but it was a step forward. It did good work for several decades. It was, for sure, better to be a Jew or a Catholic in America in 1980 rather than in 1930. It is important for us at Interfaith America both to know this history and to not repeat the mistakes of the people who made it.

The term "Judeo-Christian" did not fall from the sky or rise from the ground. It was not written on Plymouth Rock when the Pilgrims arrived on the Eastern Seaboard or discovered in the soil during the California gold rush. The term is not especially historically accurate or particularly theologically precise. Instead, "Judeo-Christian" was a concrete social response to the anti-Catholicism and anti-Semitism of the early twentieth century. It was a civic invention of one of the most impressive American civic institutions of the last one hundred years: the National Conference of Christians and Jews (NCCJ). The story is powerfully told in Kevin Schultz's excellent book *Tri-Faith America*.

The NCCJ emerged in the 1920s specifically to combat the anti-Catholic and anti-Semitic propaganda of the Ku Klux Klan. Over the course of the 1930s and 1940s, it set itself a much more ambitious mission: the creation of Judeo-Christian America, both in the public imagination and in the social infrastructure of the nation. Like the Y and the Harlem Children's Zone, the organization accomplished its mission by running a network of programs whose purpose was to instantiate their big idea. They built a board of prominent Catholics, Jews, and Protestants. They published books like *All in the Name of God*, which made the case against Protestant hegemony and for the three faiths as equal communities with much in common. NCCJ "tolerance trios," composed of clergy of the three faiths, went to cities across the nation, organizing what they termed tri-faith dialogues. The organization would then help local religious leaders in those cities put together follow-up interfaith seminars called Institutes of Human Relations. By 1941, over two hundred US cities were organizing such seminars on a regular basis, and up to two thousand smaller towns had similar ad hoc programs.

As the United States got involved in World War II, the NCCJ played a central role in creating the narrative that America was a champion of pluralism. Religiously diverse US troops fighting together exemplified the Judeo-Christian ideal of "the brotherhood of man under the fatherhood of God" combatting the evil Nazis, who were intent on destroying all diversity. (Yes, this was at the same time that lynchings were common in the US, and no, the NCCJ did not take on racism with the same zeal as they did religious bigotry—a total travesty.) NCCJ tolerance trios visited 778 different US military installations with their message of Judeo-Christian unity. They distributed millions of pamphlets and made a film called *The World We Want to Live In*, which interspersed images of ugly religious bigotry with inspiring stories of interfaith cooperation.

They were also exceptional at taking advantage of opportunities. NCCJ leaders immediately sensed the potential in the story of the Four Chaplains—two Protestant ministers, a Catholic priest, and a Jewish rabbi who gave their life jackets to frightened seamen on the sinking USS *Dorchester* and died holding hands, whispering the prayers of their respective faiths—and helped make it probably the single most potent symbol of the Judeo-Christian ideal in mid-twentieth-century America.[1]

The NCCJ made mistakes, sins of both omission and commission. They ignored virtually all other religious communities and barely engaged racism and sexism. But they made a contribution. Our job at Interfaith America is to carry their torch and not repeat their errors. There are now almost as many Muslims in America as there are Jews, and more Muslims than there are Episcopalians. It is time for a new chapter in the story of American religious diversity, a chapter titled "Interfaith America."

CHAPTER TWENTY

BE CAUTIOUS
ABOUT BECOMING A SYMBOL

THERE IS A LEGEND IN WHICH TWO CIVIL RIGHTS WORKERS have a heated discussion about the credit they are getting for their contributions to the movement. One says, "It's always Martin Luther King Jr. this and Martin Luther King Jr. that. I'm tired of hearing the name Martin Luther King Jr. What about my name? What about your name?"

The other civil rights worker responds: "Our name *is* Martin Luther King Jr."

That story, however apocryphal, illustrates the power of being a symbol. Martin Luther King Jr. was not just a container for the hopes and aspirations of civil rights workers everywhere; he was also the image of the civil rights movement to the rest of the nation. It was through watching his speeches and interviews, reading his essays, seeing photographs of him marching on the streets of Selma, that much of the nation came to embrace the cause of civil rights. He was the movement embodied in a single person.

It cost him, in the ultimate way. King was murdered because he was a symbol, not because he was a pastor.

Few people want to risk being assassinated for their cause, but I know many social change agents who are willing to take some heat in clashes with their opponents. It is the battles with friends and allies that they come to find more painful. If you choose the path of being a symbol, those battles will undoubtedly be more intense. Symbols are headlights, guiding the way. And they are targets, taking the shots.

Martin Luther King Jr. knew this battlefield well. As Taylor Branch details in his magisterial trilogy of the civil rights movement, *America in the King Years*, King's friends and colleagues were constantly tugging at him as if he were a rope—about his commitment to pacifism, about why he stayed a Christian, about why he gave queer people like Bayard Rustin a central role in the movement, about his stand on the Vietnam War, about his friendships with white people like Stanley Levison. It was a lot.[1]

You know you are in danger of becoming a symbol when other people derive their meaning from your actions, everything from what you tweet to what you wear.

The power of being a symbol is in the opportunity it gives you to serve as a vessel for other people's hopes and dreams. The hazard is that it gives other people the distinct impression that they own you.

It's instructive to consider the cases of people who embraced the role of symbol and then spurned it. Bob Dylan is a prime example.

Not long after arriving in New York City with his guitar and a handful of folk songs, Bob Dylan became the embodiment of a folk scene that held that pure acoustic music, an anti-war ideology, and personal integrity were deeply intertwined. Like a lot of orthodoxies, it seems absurd now, but I'm sure it made perfect sense at the time. In any case, Dylan became famous in part because this world embraced him as its representative, and he was happy to ride the wave to early stardom.

"Take him, he's yours," Pete Seeger said to the young crowd at the Newport Folk Festival in the early 1960s. Seeger (along with Woody Guthrie) had been the folk avatar of the previous generation. He viewed Dylan like a son, someone to be shaped in his image, passed down the line, and offered up to the adoring crowds.

Dylan was not having it. "What a crazy thing to say," Dylan reflected in his memoir, *Chronicles*. "Screw that."[2]

Dylan viewed himself as an artist first, not an ideologue, and certainly not someone bound by the dictates of other people's ideologies.

During the very same years that the white folkies had constructed him as the crystallization of their purist sensibilities, Dylan had taken to listening to electric music, from the blues to the Byrds, and dreaming up new soundscapes for his own songs.

In 1965, he shocked the Newport Folk Festival by bringing a rock band on stage and singing "Maggie's Farm," a song about refusing to subject yourself to other people's demands.

Pete Seeger threatened to cut the cord on him. Half the crowd booed.

Dylan decided he'd rather endure boos than be subject to other people's demands. He brought his electric guitar to England, took in the hisses on the other side of the Atlantic, and responded to a fan who called him Judas by saying, "I don't believe you. You're a liar." Then he turned and told his band to "play it fucking loud." They promptly went into a historic version of "Like a Rolling Stone," a song about the freedom of being unknown and on your own.

In the end, King's embrace of being a symbol helped pass civil rights legislation and change a nation. He suffered deeply for it.

Alternately, Dylan's spurning of the role of symbol allowed him to do some of his best work, including making albums that are widely considered masterpieces of American music like *Highway 61 Revisited*, *Blonde on Blonde*, and *Bringing It All Back Home*.

Being a symbol can be a highly effective strategy for a social change agent. It can also be a way to make yourself a very visible punching bag, for both your enemies and your supposed friends. It takes a nanosecond for the crowds to build you up and even less time for them to take you down.

Personally, I don't need others to derive their meaning from my identity, and I do not want to offer myself up as a canvas on which people can paint their politics. If you choose that path, just be clear-eyed about what it might cost you.

CHAPTER TWENTY-ONE

BE CAUTIOUS ABOUT MAKING GENERALIZATIONS AND SPEAKING FOR OTHERS

J UST HOURS AFTER JOE BIDEN WAS DECLARED THE VICTOR OF the 2020 presidential race, Dave Chappelle stepped onto the *Saturday Night Live* stage and called for unity. He urged his largely urban liberal audience to sympathize with rural conservative Trump voters. He identified with the experience of police officers. He pointed out that, for the first time in history, the life expectancy of white people was dropping as a result of depression, drug addiction, and suicide.

From Dave Chappelle's point of view, the problem in America was people making a show of hating one another over differences in race and politics, instead of doing our best to understand the other person's story. "*I don't hate anybody,*" Chappelle said, his voice rising with emotion. He just hated the feeling of being targeted and left out—and he didn't want anybody else to have that feeling. "You got to find a way to forgive each other," he implored his audience. We are one people, he seemed to be saying, and we all have to do our part to widen the circle.[1]

I was still moved by Chappelle's words when I clicked on a piece by Courtney Martin. I'm a regular reader of her newsletter, *The Examined Family,* because I think Courtney does such a great job of articulating the challenge of being a white professional wife and mom trying to live out progressive commitments. But this particular piece hit my frustration nerve. That she was dismissive of calls for post-election kindness, healing, and unity ("unless it is your spiritual practice") in favor of "a fiercer form of moral leadership" around "a basic agreement that racism, sexism, ableism, etc. will not be tolerated," was fine. I prefer the path forward that Dave Chappelle proposed, but I think the blatant racism, misogyny, and incompetence of the Trump years makes Courtney Martin's view totally justified.

What bothered me was that Courtney said her rejection of bridge building was done on behalf of Black people and immigrants "who have been systematically and interpersonally dehumanized by racists and xenophobes." She would not call on people of color to sympathize with those who voted differently, or build bridges, or be part of healing. In fact, she characterized such calls as "not just insensitive" but "emotionally violent" and tantamount to asking entire segments of our population to engage in "self-annihilation."[2]

But hadn't I just watched Dave Chappelle, a Black man who had built a career on dissecting virtually every painful aspect of American racism, call for unity, kindness, sympathy, and healing—and on one of the most influential stages in pop culture no less? Why was Courtney Martin assuming a kind of helplessness about people who looked like Dave Chappelle that Dave Chappelle was not assuming about himself or others who shared his racial identity? Why was Courtney Martin under the impression that the vast quantity of human beings who lived their varied lives under the labels "Black" or "immigrant" or "people of color" could so easily be characterized as sharing not just a worldview but also an emotional disposition?

A social experiment led by the psychologists Marjorie Rhodes and Sarah-Jane Leslie highlights the problem of speaking in such sweeping, stereotyping categories. In the experiment, four-year-olds were shown pictures of a diverse set of individuals (Black and white, male and female, Latinx and Asian, old and young) and told they all belonged to an identity group called the Zarpies.

The psychologists then started describing to the children what Zarpies are like. With one group of four-year-olds, the psychologists used sentences like, "Zarpies are scared of ladybugs." They called the phrases constructed in this way "generics."

With the other group of children, the psychologists spoke with more care and specificity. Instead of using a generic, they would say, "Look at *this* Zarpie! He's afraid of ladybugs."

A few days later, they showed all of the children a picture of a Zarpie and said it made buzzing sounds.

Fascinating differences emerged between the children who were previously told the generics—"Zarpies are scared of ladybugs"—and those who were not.

The children who were told the generics were quick to believe that *all* Zarpies made buzzing sounds, that this was an essential trait that Zarpies were born with, and that because all Zarpies shared some traits they would inevitably also share other traits.

In a piece in the *Huffington Post*, Rhodes summarizes the main conclusions that she and her colleagues drew from their research:

> Seemingly incongruous generic sentences, including sentences such as "girls have long hair" or "Italians love pasta[,]" . . . prepare children to develop more stereotypes . . . [and] generics can lead children to view stereotypes as inevitable and natural—to believe, for example, that girls will always dislike math, regardless of the environment they grow up in.[3]

I don't think generic language harms only children. I think it leads all of us to develop harmful stereotypes.

Here's another question: What gave Courtney the right to be the one making generalizations about people outside her social identity? It's interesting to consider the contrast between Dave Chappelle, a Black cultural icon who was calling on people to sympathize across racial and political lines, and Courtney, a white progressive writer saying Black people need to be protected from such calls because those calls are emotionally violent.

I'm friendly with Courtney, so I reached out and asked why she chose to make sweeping generalizations about the worldviews and emotions of Black people and immigrants, and in such emotionally loaded terms. She responded by sending me a powerful piece by a Black writer who found calls for unity and healing offensive. Totally justified, I believe, but how did Courtney come to the determination that *this* Black writer represented *all* people of color? And why did Courtney decide that she had license to use her own power as a white writer to declare some writers of color the voice for huge and diverse communities of people?

In his piece "The Great Awokening," Matt Yglesias notes that white liberals have so embraced the cause of anti-racism that they are further to the left on racial justice matters than both Blacks and Hispanics. For example, when asked whether they want the United States to become more diverse, only about 50 percent of Blacks and Hispanics agree, whereas closer to 90 percent of white liberals say yes. When asked whether Black people should get "special favors" to advance, *more* white liberals say yes than Black people—by something like fifteen points.[4]

People have every right to choose their politics, but no one has the right to say that their views represent the views of other groups. And yet that appears to be precisely what's happening in progressive politics these days. "America's white saviors," as the political scientist Zach Goldberg calls them, frequently advocate for positions on behalf of Black and brown people that those groups themselves do not hold. The white saviors, for example, rate "protect immigrants and their families" and "addressing race and gender issues" as extremely important on surveys, whereas the actual people of color rated "creating jobs" and "lowering taxes" as higher priorities.[5]

It's a battle that's increasingly dominating the Democratic Party. As Thomas Edsall of the *New York Times* observes, the liberal wing increasingly focuses on identity issues. The moderate wing emphasizes pocketbook issues. The liberal wing is overwhelmingly white. The moderate wing is majority people of color.[6]

Kwame Anthony Appiah, a prominent gay Black philosopher, thinks a lot of these problems can be solved if all of us committed to stop speaking for other people. In an essay titled "Go Ahead, Speak for Yourself," Appiah cautions even people *within* a particular identity category about speaking for the rest of the group. He sounded a particular warning about the formulation "as a," pointing out that it presumes a sameness within a social group that simply does not exist. Assumptions of uniformity are dangerous because everyone carries a subtle instruction to people that they need to conform to a particular definition of authenticity. When someone says that "as an immigrant" she feels dehumanized if she is called on to build bridges, she is subtly issuing a command about what the right kind of feeling the right kind of immigrant should have.

There is another problem with speaking for others, whether you are part of the group or not: it confers an authority on you that you most probably do not have. Appiah relates that he is often asked to speak as a gay man for "the gay experience." He declines. "Nobody made me head gay," he says.[7]

CHAPTER TWENTY-TWO

BE CAUTIOUS OF THE SINGLE STORY

I N A POPULAR TED TALK, THE NOVELIST CHIMAMANDA NGOZI Adichie warns of the danger of a single story, illustrating her point through a powerful personal tale.

As a middle-class family in Nigeria, the Adichies had a houseboy name Fide. Chimamanda's mother commented frequently on how poor Fide's family was and used this to encourage Chimamanda to finish her dinner and appreciate her relative comforts. When Chimamanda visited Fide's family in the village and was shown the beautiful baskets his mother made, she found herself startled. "It had not occurred to me that anybody in his family could actually make something," she said. "All I had heard about them was how poor they were, so that it had become impossible for me to see them as anything else but poor. Their poverty was my single story of them."[1]

My friend Trabian Shorters, who runs an excellent Black leaders network called BMe Community, is concerned that something similar is taking place when progressive social change agents speak about Black people. The consistent use of terms like "at-risk," "low-income," "high-crime," "high-poverty," and "disadvantaged" cannot help but create a single story about a particular population. Relying on the scholarship of industrial, social, and cognitive psychologists such as Nobel laureate Daniel Kahneman, Trabian shows that this is quintessentially stigmatizing language that, despite the good intentions, creates the image of a threat that either needs to be avoided, destroyed, or controlled.

Elijah Megginson does not want to be avoided, destroyed, controlled, or stigmatized. A high-achieving high school senior who is Black and was raised in a housing project, Elijah found himself pressured by teachers to "sell his pain" on his college application. He made a couple of half-hearted attempts, but it felt forced and fake. Elijah didn't want to be reduced to the single story of his trauma; he wanted to be known for his achievements and aspirations.

When he asked around in his circle of friends, it turned out that many of the Black high achievers had been encouraged, in everything from college application essays to classroom discussions, to emphasize only the bad things that had happened in their lives. One of his friends related how she was encouraged to speak of how terrible her life was to meet the expectations of the well-intentioned people around her. She'd wound up internalizing those stereotypes, a dynamic she felt had contributed to her low self-esteem during her college years.

The tragedy here is that adults—many of them, no doubt, well-meaning white people—are encouraging talented Black teenagers to single-story themselves. Aaron Jones, a Black teacher in New York City who attended Morehouse, is dead set against it: "The sob story can be truth, but it's not all said all."[2]

Elijah Megginson's story is a perfect illustration of my friend Trabian's point. "You can't lift people up by putting them down," is how Trabian put it in a powerful *Chronicle of Philanthropy* piece.[3] As Trabian consistently emphasizes, the focus should be first and foremost on the aspirations and achievements of Black people, and only then on the problems they face—challenges, it should be said, that are caused by structural injustices and not personal failures.

Kwame Anthony Appiah writes, "The fact that identities come without essences does not mean they come without entanglements. And the fact that they need interpreting and negotiating does not mean that each of us can do with them whatever we will."[4]

Trabian is happy to be constructively entangled in Black America. His organization, the BMe Community, is not just sounding the alarm on the challenge of single-storying an entire race, they are also embodying the change. Thousands of foundation and nonprofit leaders have experienced their Asset Framing for Equity training. I can personally attest that it is the single best training I've ever been through. BMe also has a campaign, the Next Narrative for Black America, that shows that insisting on defining Black people by their manifest aspirations to Live, Own, Vote, and Excel in America is how you build Black L.O.V.E.[5]

CHAPTER TWENTY-THREE

BE CAUTIOUS
ABOUT THE FALSE SOCIAL MAP

I T'S EASY TO TELL WHEN A MAP OF THE PHYSICAL WORLD IS false. If the street names on the map don't align with the names on the actual street signs, we know the map is wrong. If I ask you directions to a coffee shop and you tell me to take a left at the corner and walk down two blocks, and I do it only to find that there's no coffee shop there, I know the map you are using is off.

Whereas a map of the physical world notes street names, city boundaries, and the locations of buildings, a map of the social world labels the categories of various population groups, fills in their views and experiences, and plots them in relation to one another.

To assign your preferred politics to your favored groups even when they object, to give people labels they don't use for themselves, to pretend that imagined categories that are incoherent to begin with actually have hard-and-fast boundaries—all of this leads to the creation of a false social map. And you cannot build things on a false social map.

Look closely at the category "people of color." Taken globally, it would easily include over 80 percent of the human race (virtually everybody outside of Europe, North America, New Zealand, and Australia, and of course many of the people within those societies as well). Are there any generalizations that can be usefully made about this many people? Even just considered within the United States, the category "people of color" lacks coherence. Indian Americans are the highest earning ethnic group in the United States, Somali Americans the lowest earning. They might both have more pigment in their skin than people with Irish or Polish ancestry, but they are very unlikely to live in the same neighborhood. To assume that they do is to insist on a false social map.

Or consider the label "Latinx," now used almost ubiquitously in progressive circles. However, only 3 percent of people of Hispanic heritage say they prefer the term for themselves. *Fewer than 25 percent say they have even heard the word.*[1]

If you give someone bad directions based on a false physical map, you could get them lost. The same goes for a false social map. Let's say you are involved in a political campaign, and you are trying to craft policies and messages to get a particular candidate elected. You send your organizers to a neighborhood with a large number of people who trace their ancestry back to Mexico, Cuba, and Puerto Rico. Those organizers persist in referring to the people who answer their doors as "part of the Latinx community," but those people have either never heard the phrase or don't like it, so they are less likely to vote for your candidate. If your political commercials and mailings emphasize a message of distrust for the police to a community that actually wants more cops in their neighborhood rather than fewer, they are less likely to vote for your candidate. If you do all of this while assuring the community that you are doing it *on their behalf* because *you know their identity better than they do*, you are not only likely to lose votes in that election; you are also likely to leave them feeling deeply insulted and thus will turn them off of your message for a long time.

Some version of this may well have happened in the 2020 election, and not just with respect to the Latinx/Hispanic community. If ever a social map that singularly emphasized the message of anti-racism was going to turn out non-white voters, it was going to be 2020. Donald Trump was a man who spoke of Mexicans as rapists, Muslims as terrorists, Chinese people as diseased, and Black people as violent. And yet Trump received more votes across virtually every non-white group in 2020 than he did in 2016. The one group Trump received fewer votes from in 2020 was white men.

The sociologist Musa Al-Gharbi did not mince words in his characterization of the situation: "There's hardly a better indication of Democrats' inability to speak to ordinary people about things they care about than this—that in the midst of the milieu we find ourselves in [recession, pandemic, racial justice protests], they still lost minority voters."[2]

According to a comprehensive post-election autopsy by Third Way, the Collective PAC, and Latino Victory, the social map used by Republicans turned out to be more accurate than the one used by Democrats. The Republican Party paid attention to the intricate diversities within broader categories like Hispanic. They did not assume that the entire community would be principally moved by a single message or ideology and instead designed specific approaches to different communities—one for Cuban Americans in Florida and another for Mexican Americans in the Rio Grande Valley, for example. This was smart strategy, much truer to the actual identities of people than the imagined ones. The Democrats, by contrast, basically treated the entire Latinx community as a single category and believed that they would be swayed if the party emphasized the evils of racism loudly enough.[3]

The political strategist David Shor points out the obvious: if such trends continue, it would be the Republicans who are on the way to putting together the multiracial, working-class political coalition that progressives say is so important to us.[4]

If progressives want to build either civic institutions or political coalitions, we will need to design—and use—an accurate social map.

CHAPTER TWENTY-FOUR

BE CAUTIOUS
WHEN ACCUSING OTHERS

I WAS IN A BAD MOOD. I'D MISSED THE LAST FLIGHT FROM LOS
Angeles to Chicago the night before, creating havoc in my work
schedule. My wife was leaving on her own trip that day, causing stress
in my household. To top it all off, it was raining, and the early morning shuttle to the airport was running late.

I stood right behind the scrum of people waiting to board and
scrolled impatiently through my phone. If I had been paying closer
attention, I would have probably noticed that there were more people
standing outside than there were seats on the bus. Maybe I would
have tried to work my way to the front of the line, but I was too distracted to put in the effort. Plus, I'd actually signed up for the 6 a.m.
shuttle with the overnight desk clerk. I figured all I needed to do was
wait for the driver to call my name.

But instead of shouting out names, the driver started calling people by numbers. I think someone mentioned something about the
sign-up sheet being lost. By the time I put my phone away and looked
up, the shuttle was full.

"Hey, what the hell," I said out loud. A bad morning was about to
turn into a terrible day. My wife was going to be furious if I missed
this flight. To add insult to injury, every person sitting in the shuttle
seemed to be a white guy dressed in khakis and a polo. It looked like
a racist conspiracy, and my top just blew off.

I stepped onto the shuttle, waved my arms to get everyone's attention and shouted: "I think it is blatantly racist that everyone on the shuttle is white and the one person who gets left off has brown skin."

Then I pointed at the driver and said, "And you are the person most responsible."

The white guys on the bus all stared down at their phones. Nobody offered to give up their seat for me (why should they?), but no one came to the defense of the driver either. A public charge of racism? Better not to get involved.

The driver, a white woman with unkempt gray hair, stared at me, a look of terror crossing her face. She got out of her seat, walked inside the hotel, and started frantically talking to the desk clerk. I couldn't tell exactly what she was saying, but she looked like she was about to cry.

I regretted the accusation as soon as it came out of my mouth. To begin with, it was false, or at least hollow. There was not a shred of evidence that this woman had deliberately excluded me because of my race. If I had been paying attention during the loading process, I could have probably told her that I really needed to be on this shuttle, indeed that I had signed up the night before. I have no doubt that I would have been accommodated.

As I watched the driver talking to the desk clerk, looking more and more desperate with every word, my regret turned to guilt. I had not accused an abstract entity of racism; I had accused a real person of it. Yes, my frustration had boiled over. But there was another reason I had made the charge: I knew that it would have power.

In fact, the situation is something of a case study in power dynamics. I have an excellent job with a high salary and good benefits. This woman made maybe $15 an hour. Moreover, I work frequently with corporate executives and relate well to them. We went to the same schools, live in the same neighborhoods, put our kids in the same enrichment programs. If I chose to summon my class privilege and escalate the issue, it could mean her job. A public charge of racism by someone like me, a member of the meritocratic elite, can have a kind of nuclear power. It can destroy someone's life, or at least cost a person her job. And a hotel shuttle driver is eminently expendable.

The driver knew this, too, which is why she was inside the hotel trying desperately to get the desk clerk to vouch for her in case I followed through on my accusation and made a complaint to her boss.

Accusations have power. When Oumou Kanoute, a Black student at Smith College, leveled the charge of racism against employees who asked her to stop eating her lunch in a dorm that was closed to Smith students for the summer, it did not turn out well for the employees of the college.

Ms. Kanoute said that the situation left her near "meltdown" and claimed that "her existence overall as a woman of color" was being questioned.[1] The employees said they were just doing their job, which included keeping Smith students out of a dormitory that was reserved for a summer camp.

After Ms. Kanoute put the accusation on Facebook, Smith's president, Kathleen McCartney, came to her immediate defense, releasing this statement: "This painful incident reminds us of the ongoing legacy of racism and bias in which people of color are targeted while simply going about the business of their ordinary lives." Several national media outlets picked up the story and told it from Ms. Kanoute's perspective. The American Civil Liberties Union also defended Ms. Kanoute, claiming that she was being accused of "eating while Black."

I am in favor of taking seriously allegations of racism and the subjective experiences of people of color. I am also, generally speaking, in favor of the kind of enhanced diversity training that President McCartney mandated for the staff of Smith College in the wake of the accusation.

But I think all of this could have been accomplished without destroying the lives of the accused employees. President McCartney put the janitor, a man in his sixties with failing eyesight, on paid leave the day Ms. Kanoute posted her accusation on Facebook. Jackie Blair, a food service employee who had also reminded Ms. Kanoute of the rule against eating in the dorm, had her life changed forever.

"This is the racist person," Ms. Kanoute wrote about Ms. Blair on Facebook. Suddenly, Ms. Blair was the target of an anti-racist campaign. People called her at her home accusing her of being a racist. She found notes in her mailbox and taped to her car window. "You don't deserve to live," one of them read.

Ms. Blair makes $40,000 a year, on a campus where tuition and fees run to nearly $80,000 per year. The stress caused complications of her lupus, which required hospital treatment. Also, there was serious psychological torment. "Oh my God, I didn't do this," she told a friend. "I exchanged a hello with that student and now I'm being called a racist."

The administration did not defend Ms. Blair. What they did do was hire a law firm that specializes in discrimination investigations to look closely into the incident. The firm issued a report, which cleared every individual accused of racism: Ms. Blair, two janitors, and a security officer.

But by then, the damage had been done. "Four people's lives wrecked, two were employees of more than 35 years and no apology. . . . We were gobsmacked," said Tracy Putnam Culver, a Smith graduate who once worked for facilities management at the college.

Ms. Blair spent another couple of years at Smith, occasionally overhearing students point her out as the racist one. She was let go by the college in the fall of 2020 because of the coronavirus pandemic. When she applied for an hourly job at a local restaurant, the manager set up a Zoom interview and questioned her about her involvement in the racist incident at Smith.

"What do I do?" she wondered. "When does this racist label go away?"

Rashaan Hall, racial justice director for the ACLU of Massachusetts, served as Ms. Kanoute's lawyer. He dismissed the conclusion of the report, pointing out that implicit racial bias is frequently at play in dynamics between white people and people of color but is hard to prove outright.

I can see that point of view. I've been in plenty of rooms where I was one of a handful of people of color in a sea of whiteness, and I know well the dis-ease of those situations. The accumulated frustration can build and build. It partially explains why I exploded while staring at that shuttle full of smug white guys in khakis. I can absolutely see how Ms. Kanoute might have felt cornered while eating her lunch and being confronted by several white people, even though there is no dispute that she was breaking the rules by being in the dormitory in the first place.

What I do not understand is why Mr. Hall adamantly refused to sympathize with the Smith employees who were the targets of Ms. Kanoute's accusations. "Allegations of being racist, even getting direct mailers in their mailbox, is not on par with the consequences of actual racism," he told the *New York Times*. But what if you were not being racist, and you get publicly shamed for it anyway? What if it affects your job, your reputation, your mental health, your physical health?

There have been enough such incidents for Anne Applebaum to write a major piece in *The Atlantic* titled "The New Puritans" on the subject. Applebaum reviewed dozens of cases of people (mostly professors and writers) who had been accused of racism or sexism but had not been formally charged with an actual crime. A pattern quickly became clear. The accused were investigated by their workplace under a presumption of guilt rather than innocence and without much by way of due process. Friends and colleagues stopped talking to them. The accused found they could no longer function in their jobs. Depression, a crisis of identity, and suicidal ideation were common. A few actually killed themselves. These are not minor inconveniences. These are significant, life-altering consequences.

Throughout her article, Applebaum, a writer not known for hyperbole, made frequent comparisons to the witch hunts of the Puritan era and the culture of fear cultivated by totalitarian regimes. "Right here in America, right now, it is possible to meet people who have lost everything—jobs, money, friends, colleagues—after violating no laws and sometimes no workplace rules either," she writes.[2] What's worse, the investigating authorities are typically not the government's secret police but rather the institutions that are supposed to be most committed to an open society: colleges and universities, magazines and newspapers, think tanks and advocacy organizations like the ACLU.

My own story ended with a whimper rather than a bang. The next shuttle came early; I took my seat and put my headphones on. The driver of the first shuttle walked past and averted her eyes, but I could still detect the fear on her face. A moment of frustration for me could have been the end of a job for her. Maybe worse. Even though the incident occurred years ago, I can't put it out of my mind. Why did I reach for the gun of accusation so easily? Why did it strike such fear in a person who did no wrong?

Actual racism can wreck lives. Hollow accusations can do the same.

A LETTER TO MY SONS, FUTURE BUILDERS OF DIVERSE DEMOCRACY

DEAR ZAYD AND KHALIL,
Here's what a dad on Khalil's baseball team said to me the other day: "On the way back from practice, our boys were having the best conversation about religion, and Khalil was leading it."

Had he told me, Khalil, that you had pitched a perfect game *and* hit a grand slam, I don't think I would have been more proud. I mean, there are kids all over the country who can play baseball. What the nation really needs is youth with interfaith leadership skills.

I wanted the story directly from the hero himself. That's why I asked you about it, Khalil.

You told me that you wanted to know how Ian and Scott did their prayers, and what their religious holidays were like, and where they went to worship. You said that Scott is Jewish and Ian is Christian.

I asked you what you told them about our religion, and you said, "Nothing."

Nothing? You didn't say that we pray together as a family every night, or talk about Eid or jamat khana, or the Qur'an or the Aga Khan? *Nothing?*

I was confused, so you explained it to me.

"Dad," you said, clearly trying to be patient with me, "Christians and Jews are basically the same. They're like, *Americans.* Muslims are not like Christians and Jews. *Muslims are different.* Plus, I'm brown.

Christians and Jews are white. I thought it was just better to be the one asking the questions and let them do the talking."

I was absolutely flabbergasted. A neighborhood dad had told me that you were leading a conversation about religion in the back seat of his car, a story that I had interpreted *as a sign of your confidence in your identity.* I apologize. I should have known better. I should have known how racism seeps through even the most protected environments, especially when it had a champion in the White House in the form of Donald Trump.

I grew up with my own challenges in this area. I knew full well that when I was around the age you boys are now, losing a tetherball game could earn me a set of racist taunts. Of course, winning a tetherball game against one of the popular kids might provoke the same. I was always threading that needle.

I knew that when a recent immigrant with a strong Indian accent arrived in my math class halfway through seventh grade, I needed to be the first one who bullied him, thus establishing my distance from the alien and making clear that I stood on the right side of the line, the one labeled normal (the inside tag listed the ingredients: white, Christian, American).

Boys, I am embarrassed to tell you that the things I encourage you to do now—to go out of your way to bring the kid on the sidelines into the game, to be an upstander and not a bystander—I did virtually none of when I was your age. My brown skin already made me a target; why would I go out of my way to invite more abuse?

I don't want to pretend that nothing has changed since I was a kid. Barack Obama was elected president twice and is still among the most popular political figures in the United States. A significant number of the books that you are assigned in school have minority lead characters. *Way* more than half of your pop culture heroes—mostly hip-hop artists, YouTube personalities, and athletes—are Black and brown.

That is *progress.*

And still racism seeps in.

Zayd, remember when we walked by the Old Town School of Folk Music and I was so excited to point out the poster for the band Tinariwen? I told you it was a group that played West African roots music and that a lot of the artists were Muslim. You looked at the poster, featuring men wearing long robes and head wraps against a desert backdrop, and said, "Dad, that's ISIS."

I mean, it was a poster at a concert venue. I had just told you they were a band that your mom and I had gone to see. But what you saw was dark men against a desert dressed in robes and the word "Muslim," and your instinctive association was "terrorist." That's the racism from the broader culture seeping into your personal system.

The truth is, your mother and I play a part in this. Remember when we were selling our house? We didn't cook Indian food the entire time. Zayd, you didn't even ask why not. You knew. One evening you actually put it into words. You said you missed chicken curry but that you understood that Indian food smells strong and that it might turn potential buyers off. Your contribution to the discussion was to suggest we take the Qur'an calendar down. Your reasoning was sound. If the smell of Indian food might turn some people off, certainly the verses of the Qur'an on prominent display could do the same.

All foods smell. We didn't worry about cooking burgers or preparing spaghetti with meatballs, did we? And all homes are decorated with symbols of meaning, often religious ones. Why did we feel like we needed to hide *our* food and *our* religious symbols?

Right now, you both see these things as just part of life, just as I saw walking the fine line between not losing too badly and not winning too obviously in tetherball as just part of life. The kids who run faster have an easier time in sports than the kids who run slower. The kids with brown skin and Muslim names navigate the world differently—they don't talk about their family's prayer practices with friends, they don't cook their favorite food when they are trying to sell their house—than the kids with white skin and "normal" names. But if your journey is anything like mine, you might get to college and read Audre Lorde or Andrea Dworkin or bell hooks and realize that there is a language for these things: racism, privilege, implicit bias, white supremacy, double consciousness. You will realize that when you looked at brown people on a concert poster and immediately thought "terrorist," that was the poison of racism in the broader culture, and it was silently choking you. Worse, it was making you choke yourself.

And then, if you are anything like me, you will rage.

I remember my own period of rage as if it was yesterday. That's because, for me at least, understanding the social phenomenon of racism was a deeply personal journey. I had to come to terms with how it had deformed me. How I had secretly resented my parents for visiting their skin color on me. How I had refused to learn Indian languages, or even for a time get close to extended family, because that would only mark me as more alien. The fear I felt on the Sunday nights when the character Apu made an appearance on *The Simpsons*, knowing that I would be met with a set of "Eboo is a Slurpee maker" chants on the playground the next morning.

And yet, what did the rage accomplish? I suppose it is a natural reaction, but not an especially useful one. My Buddhist friends like to say that getting angry is like drinking poison and hoping your enemy will die.

I drank the poison, nobody died, but I got very sick in the process. Part of that sickness was *wanting* people to die—not literally, of course, but as viscerally as you can get and still be in the realm of metaphor. In the course of my journey, I met some people who thought that raging was the only way to create social change. That's not true, and I'm glad for it. I'm not suggesting that rage has *never* been a part of creating positive change, I'm only saying that it's hard to build with, and also that it's not for me. The brand of social change I've always found more inspiring is the kind that seeks the best for everyone, including the people you consider your enemies.

I think this is the great genius of Martin Luther King Jr. King realized that, in a democracy, *you have to live with the people you defeat.* They get to vote, to advocate for their views, to amass power, to do all the things that you get to do. If you say that the new world you are building has no place for them, why would they journey with you to that place? If you insist that they will never rise above their worst qualities, how will they ever know they have better ones, let alone aspire to embody those?

My message to you, Zayd and Khalil: tell a story of America where we all belong; build civic spaces where we can all contribute and feel connected. You want people who are being their worst selves to be their better selves. And truthfully, you want to be better too. All of us need to be better.

Do you remember the first demonstration that your mother and I took you to? It was the fifty-year commemoration of Martin Luther King Jr.'s march through the South Side neighborhood of Marquette Park. Do you know what King endured that day? *Five thousand people lined the streets of the neighborhood to scream racist slurs and throw bottles and bricks at King and a few hundred peaceful marchers.* A brick hit King in the head, he went down on a knee, wiped the blood away, stood up, and kept marching. At one point, King saw a pack of white teenagers screaming racist slurs on the sidewalk. Somehow, he escaped his security detail, approached the kids, and said something to the effect of, "You guys are so smart and good looking, why would you want to act this way?"[1]

Today, Marquette Park is one of the most ethnically diverse neighborhoods on the South Side. The demonstration we went to was organized by an organization called the Inner-City Muslim Action Network. As part of the commemoration, they erected the first permanent memorial to Martin Luther King Jr. in the city of Chicago. The memorial has quotes from Muslim and Jewish leaders who were looking to build the same kind of world that King was trying to build, a world where everybody thrives.

Parenting is in no small part the process of praying that your kids get right the things you got wrong. So allow me this hope. You will acquire the radar screen to detect racism, the language to deconstruct it, the structural soundness to not be deformed by it, and the leadership skills to transform it without a detour down the road of rage. Instead, you will maintain the hopefulness of King, of Lincoln, of John Lewis, of Jane Addams. Because here's the thing: if it was not for them, our family would not be in this country. It is precisely because they imagined a nation based on shared ideals rather than shared ethnicity, a nation where avowed racists could change, that new laws were passed in the 1960s that allowed your grandparents to immigrate to this nation. Those people paved a path for you: it is your job to pave a path for others. To paraphrase T. S. Eliot, *We do not inherit traditions; we work to make ourselves worthy of them.*[2] You are Americans. The tradition of America is a glorious tradition, built by sweat and blood, and art and poetry. What will you do to make yourself worthy of it?

We might have been navigating people's unconscious racial bias, perhaps even a deeply rooted form of white supremacy, when we were selling our house, but just remember, *we had a house to sell, and we were moving into one we liked better.* Both of you have known nothing but nice houses, safe neighborhoods, and excellent schools. You think this is the way the whole world is. Khalil, I remember the time you saw a story on the local news about a shooting in Chicago. You turned to me and said, "Wait, Dad, people in Chicago get shot?"

You and your friends talk about which college you want to go to, not whether you think you might go to college. That's in part because virtually every one of *their* parents went to college, and just about all of them have plum positions in the knowledge economy. The data shows that three-quarters of their children—your friends—will earn college degrees by the time they are twenty-four. That's not because they are more brilliant than the rest of the country and the world, that's because they—and you—are more privileged.

I say all this because one of the things that strikes me about the fancy colleges you both want to attend is that they are the ones that are most likely to teach you a language of criticism and deconstruction, a language that encourages you to think of yourself as oppressed.

I think this is a useful pair of glasses to put on from time to time, but it's a terrible idea to do permanent surgery on your eyes such that you only see the bad things that happen to you.

First of all, you are not oppressed. To use that word in reference to yourself is to announce to the world that you utterly lack perspective. Most of the world would trade places with you in an instant.

I learned this, as I learned many things, by the way of maximum embarrassment.

I remember being in a taxi in Mumbai with my own father. I was on a break from graduate school at Oxford and reflecting out loud on how challenging I found the environment. "It's a place that built the empire, and now it has to deal with the people it colonized returning as its students. It doesn't know how to treat us as equals, and so it oppresses us through other means."

I was proud of my postcolonial analysis, especially given the backdrop of India. Not only was I challenging the empire; I was also expressing solidarity with my countrymen. My dad did not see it the same way. He pointed to a child on the street, probably eight years old, missing his right arm and with a horrible scar on the side of his face, his left hand extended toward our window, begging for money. I had not noticed him. There were so many others who looked similar that I had learned quickly to ignore them. "If you are oppressed, what word do you have for him?" my dad asked. "*For all of them,*" he said with emphasis, pointing to the many other leprous beggars on the streets.

I didn't have an answer. I still don't.

A few years later, I had something of a similar experience. I was complaining to an Islamic scholar from the Middle East about the policies of the Bush administration. Something about the way I was talking conveyed a kind of self-pity that apparently put him off.

"Where will you sleep tonight?" he asked me.

"In my bed," I said, a little confused. "Why do you ask?"

"Because I just want you to realize that if you were in my country and you said such things about its leader, you would not be sleeping in your bed tonight, you would be in jail being tortured. You

Americans should have greater appreciation for your freedoms and spend more time doing things for other people rather than feeling sorry for yourselves."

The term "oppression," if it means anything at all, cannot include *both* upper-middle-class brown kids in urban America *and* people who sleep on the filthy streets or in the torture chambers of developing world nations.

Here is the bottom line: I do not want you to feel like the *only* story to tell about your brown skin, ethnic heritage, and Muslim faith is a story of marginalization, as if being Indian or Muslim are categories absent of content of their own, defined only by experiences of racism. I want you to realize how much progress has been made and to be grateful to all the people who did the work and made the sacrifices from which you benefit. The "we are even worse off now than we were during segregation or colonialism" narrative is not only a lie; it also dishonors the genuine heroes who fought, bled, and in some cases died to build a nation where most of us live better lives.

I want you to have the radar screen to recognize racism and the tools to call it out and to also realize that such accusations are serious and ought not be made lightly. I don't want you to go hunting for examples of racism and white supremacy. There is enough of it in the world already. Generally, I'd like you to give people the benefit of the doubt. For example, most ignorant questions about Islam are not examples of racism, but rather illustrations of being uninformed, and therefore are opportunities to do some good by providing a little education. By the way, you will undoubtedly say some uninformed things about other people's identities, and you will appreciate when they gently correct your misunderstanding rather than zap you with an accusation.

I have some counterintuitive advice for you: *embrace your privilege.* Not in a way that makes you self-satisfied (you did nothing to earn your privileges) or complacent, but in a "I have great potential, opportunity, and responsibility" manner. Whatever might be wrong with the world or challenging about your own life, I want your first instinct to be, "What can I do to be a better person, change agent, and leader?" That doesn't mean that *other people* don't need to change, it only means that if you are going to be the person leading that change, you need to be a better version of yourself. The first step toward that is understanding yourself as an agent and not a victim.

One of my favorite mantras is from the field of community organizing: don't do for people what they can do for themselves. The message is clear—people are infinitely powerful, and your job as a community organizer is to help them see their own power and then put that power into the world. Zayd and Khalil, I want you to apply that lesson to yourselves.

This is a lesson you know really well because you both play sports. *Every coach you've had has emphasized at every practice and in every game: focus on being a better person, player, and teammate. Don't make excuses.*

Zayd, I remember coming early to pick you up from basketball practice one day and getting to watch the scrimmage. The point guard got his shot blocked and yelled, out of frustration, "I'm too short."

He's right, I thought. He *is* short—a serious disadvantage in basketball.

That's not the way your coach saw it. *He was furious.* He yelled, "We *never* talk about the things we can't do or the things we don't have. We *never* make excuses. We work hard, we improve, we commit to excellence." Your coach at the time, Renell, was a walking example of this. He was short himself, well under six feet. And yet he'd made it to the NBA D-League. How? He did what he could with what he had. Those are the highest values of athletics and of leadership in general.

Remember when our flight to Arizona was delayed by ten hours and we were stuck at Midway Airport all day? The only consolation was that the people sitting next to us were players from an AAU school basketball team. I loved how you peppered those young men with questions about how they got to be elite athletes.

I'll never forget that conversation. The point guard on the team motioned over to a middle-aged Black man reading a newspaper.

"That's our coach," the player said. "He makes us do drills over and over. He has us run every time we make a mistake. He doesn't give out many compliments. He always says that he makes practices harder than games so that by the time we get there, we find the game easy."

The player looked directly at you two and said, "You prepare like that, and you become mentally tough enough to deal with anything."

You see similar themes in just about every sports-related commercial on television. Think about that Nike ad that features all those people with no hands and legs, kids from villages in developing nations and urban ghettoes—all of whom make it to the top of their field. Unfairness is at the center of the narrative. But the message is not to point out all the ways that the system (or in this case, the sport) is structured against you. The message is to adopt an attitude that overcomes disadvantage through your own excellence.[3]

Here's my favorite part of that commercial: it's narrated by Colin Kaepernick. Kaep, as you both well know, started the protest movement of kneeling during the national anthem that has now become a mainstay of athletic events. He narrated that Nike ad to send a message that unfair and oppressive systems are not going to prevent him from doing the work to achieve excellence. He's still ready to play at the highest level.

That's the great wisdom of sports.

The game is hard, your opponent is strong, you are disadvantaged—all of this is assumed. Away games are meant to be hostile territory, not safe spaces. Prepare for it. The other team will try to trigger you. Be mentally strong. Microaggressions? Laugh at them. And learn to channel your own macro-aggression into excellence. Work harder. Dig deeper.

Just about every coach I've ever been around has preached some version of this message. It should not go unnoticed that people from marginalized populations thrive in these settings. Both the NBA and the NFL are approximately three-quarters African American. Major League Baseball is nearly 50 percent Latino. In the process of thriving, those Black and brown athletes changed entire sports. Basketball is a radically different and far more exciting game, from the style of play to fashion styles, now that Black players dominate rather than white players.

This is not just a recipe for excellence in athletics. I remember sitting next to the great Black artist Kerry James Marshall at a dinner once. He spoke to me about the tragedy of so many vacant lots on the South and West Sides of Chicago. What do those vacant lots tell young Black people about their worth in the world?

In so many ways, he told me, his art is a response to those vacant lots. Its goal is to show Black people as complex, beautiful, satisfied, complete. He paints Black hairdressers, Black magicians, Black lovers, Black siblings, Black painters, Black people vacationing on a boat. He is creating an entire Black universe standing on a foundation of its own strength. The color black in his paintings always stands on its own; it is never mixed in with any other colors.

He makes it clear in a video called *Mastry* that he is not angry at the old masters for their white ways. That Rubens was painting fleshy naked blond women was *his* world and *his* era. Marshall's view is some version of "Fine, whatever, that was how *you* saw things. It's not worth my precious time to critique it."[4]

Kerry James Marshall wants to spend all of his time on a different goal: to give Black Americans what *they* deserved by painting *their world* at the very highest level of excellence. And if he found himself unable to do that, Marshall was not going to blame Rubens or any other dead white man for that. "That's *my* problem to solve," he said. And if he could not find a solution, then what he had on his hands was a failure of imagination, not a reason to blame someone else.

Kerry James Marshall was not going to let the limits of others limit him. Neither was Lori Lightfoot, the gay Black woman who grew up working class in a small town and rose to become mayor of Chicago. On the night of her election, Lightfoot was interviewed by Lisa Desjardins of PBS and asked what her mother said when she heard the good news. Here's how the mayor-elect responded: "My mother basically said, 'This is how I raised you. To be strong and fearless. To meet challenges, to take advantage of opportunities, to prepare yourself to be in charge.'"[5]

Imagine being a Black girl born when much of the United States was still segregated. Your parents work multiple jobs to make ends meet. You are slowly recognizing that your sexuality doesn't fit the norm, but it's not something you can share because of the homophobia deeply woven into the culture, especially in your small Midwestern town. And your mom tells you to be strong and fearless, to meet challenges, take advantage of opportunities, and prepare yourself to lead.

You are fully aware of the race, gender, class, and sexuality advantages that other people have. You notice it in college at the University of Michigan, in law school at the University of Chicago, as a young lawyer in the district attorney's office, as a more experienced attorney at the corporate law firm Mayer Brown, in your various appointed governmental positions. There are a whole bunch of people who, on account of their skin color, gender, family background, and so on seem as if they dropped from the sky onto third base, and when friends rig the system so they can saunter home, they act impressed with themselves.

And here you are, smarter and more focused than all of them, just meeting challenges, taking advantage of opportunities, and preparing to be in charge.

And now you are the mayor of Chicago. And you know who is not surprised? Your mother.

Speaking of mothers, yours is remarkable. Easily the best thing that happened in my life was meeting and marrying her. If you want to talk about privileges, having a mom like yours tops the list.

Right now you mostly see her as someone who drives you places, helps you with homework, and says yes to about half your requests for sleepovers. But you should know a few other things too. Your mom was a civil rights attorney who handled mostly police misconduct cases. She argued fourteen cases in federal court and was the lead attorney on two appellate arguments.

Police misconduct is a euphemism for when cops brutalize people. It's been all in the news these last few years. Names like Laquan

McDonald, Philando Castile, Michael Brown, Sandra Bland, Eric Garner, George Floyd, *and way too many others* have become part of the national discourse. Well, your mom cared about these issues long before they led the evening news. That's because your mom cares about people—all people. That includes the people who hurt the clients she was defending. Yes, I mean the police.

When your mom and I were dating and I was learning more about her work trying police misconduct cases (and falling in love with her at the same time), I made a disparaging remark about cops.

She looked at me as if I'd said something profane. "I do what I do to return dignity to people who have been violated and to help police officers live up to the code they swear to: to serve and protect. Police officers have important and difficult jobs. If I do *my* work right, they do *their* jobs better, and that is good for everyone."

Here's the thing, Zayd and Khalil: your mom doesn't think in us/ them terms, even when so many people around her do. She's on everybody's side, all the time.

I want you to be like that, looking to build things, not just tearing them down. I would be proud of you if after the killing of Michael Brown, you were in Ferguson protesting a racist criminal justice system. But I'd be prouder still if you were the ones taking responsibility to improve the police department in Ferguson. Doesn't every community deserve a decent police department—or even better, alternatives that secure public safety and community thriving without any threat of violence? Isn't that what the protestors are calling for? Somebody's got to take charge of implementing the solution. Why not you?

The final and maybe most important thing I have to say to you: let your religion be a source of strength. You might find times in your life when it is *the* source of strength.

Religion plays a strange role in identity discussions these days. Some diversity progressives view it as part of the problem, citing stats like white Evangelical Christians were Donald Trump's most rabidly loyal base. They are not wrong about this. Other diversity progressives are happy to ridicule religion, even as they champion other dimensions of identity.

I know a coffee shop that aggressively promotes its embrace of all identities. The staff is multiracial and of every conceivable sexuality and gender expression; the clientele equally so.

But when it comes to religion, the embrace grows cold. "Happy Zombie Jesus," one of the staff said breezily last April. Those of us in the space looked at her quizzically. "It's Easter Sunday," she said. Her voice took a sarcastic turn—"Jesus has risen"—then back to breezy. "So I call it Zombie Jesus Day."

The ones who laughed did it loudly. Contempt for religion was a badge to be worn with pride. Those with pain on their faces, the ones who believed that Jesus's rising meant that God had sent him as a savior, kept quiet.

You already know about the set of Americans who are immediately suspicious of you because of your Muslim faith. The strange thing about the times we live in is that the type of people who joke about "Zombie Jesus Day" may well *embrace* you when they find out you're Muslim. That's because they are opposed to discrimination, and Islamophobia is a form of discrimination. And yes, they are discriminating against Christians at the same time; adults can be very peculiar.

I think it's a good thing to hate Islamophobia, but I want the basis of your Muslim identity to be love of Islam.

As I have emphasized to you over and over again in our daily Qur'an readings and discussions, Islam is about monotheism and mercy, and for Muslims they are deeply linked.

God creates us, makes us his *abd* and *khalifa* (servant and representative), gives us responsibility to steward creation, and commands us above all to do it in the spirit of mercy. Remember my favorite line from the Qur'an, the one that I can barely utter whole without tearing up: "God sent you to be nothing but a special mercy upon all the worlds."

And you remember our lesson on Sura 93, especially the context in which it came to the Prophet Muhammad? God had generously given the Prophet revelation beginning in the month of Ramadan in the year 610. And then suddenly, without warning, the revelation stopped. God had ceased His communication and the Prophet felt forlorn, bereft.

And then Sura 93 comes crashing through the sky. It opens with God reminding the Prophet that He has by no means abandoned him. God gives him a promise: "What is to come is better for you / than what has come before." And then God gives him a reminder:

> *"Did He not find you an orphan*
> *and take care of you?*
> *Did He not find you poor*
> *And enrich you?"*

And God gives the Prophet a task:

> *"So do not oppress the orphan,*
> *And do not drive*
> *The beggar away."*

God ends the Sura with this:

> *"And keep recounting the favours of your Lord."*

This is, in my view, the wisdom of Islam in a few short lines. God is with you, always. What He has done for you is beyond imaginable. These gifts that He has given you—support, guidance, sustenance—you must give to others. And you must do it with a spirit of gratitude, because the Source of all things has given you strength.

I think this is the verse that Mos Def must have been thinking about when he wrote the lyrics to "Fear Not of Man."[6] People too often think that they're valuable because of their good looks or their piles of money. But that's a lie. People are valuable and powerful because they have been created by God.

I want you to feel throughout your being that you are cosmically, eternally valuable. That God created you to be *His* vicegerent on

His creation. That when God created our common ancestor Prophet Adam, the first human being, the representative of all humankind, the Angels ridiculed Adam and told God that he would only fiddle and destroy. God responded: "I know what you do not know." *God vouched for our goodness in the face of the Angels' denial.* And then God gave us a gift—the ability to say the names of His Creation. This is a gift that the Angels did not receive; it is the gift that distinguishes human beings from every other blessed creature that God has created.

Look at that word: *names.* Do you see that it is plural, not singular? God's Creation is not a monoculture; it is full of diversity. *The gift that God has given especially to us is the ability to flow with diversity.*

And now perhaps you understand why I so proudly call myself an American Muslim, and why I hope you do too. Because in the purest parts of both traditions, there is a cherishing of diversity and a recognition of its holiness.

A final story from Islam.

In the year 628, while he was living in Medina and right after he had fought a series of defensive wars against the Meccan tribes who were threatened by the coming of Islam, the Prophet has a dream. He is returning to Mecca, and he is coming not as a warrior but as a pilgrim.

This is a dream, the Prophet thinks to himself, given to me by God.

The next morning the Prophet wakes and explains the dream to his companions. He commands them to drop their weapons, to dress in the all-white garb of the pilgrim, and to ride in a state of *ihram*, an enveloping meditative spiritual approach to the world. They ride to a small roundabout right outside the city of Mecca called Hudaybiyyah, where they are met by Suhayl, a commander of the most belligerent of the Meccan tribes. Suhayl knows that he is caught in a bind. It was part of the Meccan custom to protect all communities doing the pilgrimage, but there was no way he was going to allow these sworn enemies into the city. The Prophet agreed to negotiate a settlement.

Even though the Prophet is in a stronger position, he does not negotiate especially aggressively. In fact, the Treaty of Hudaybiyyah records him basically giving away the store. The Muslims will repatriate the prisoners they have captured and do so without demanding reciprocity. Anyone who has converted and moved to Medina but now wishes to rethink their conversion and return home to their family in Mecca is free to do so. Again, no reciprocity is required. Most striking of all, the Prophet assents to leaving without performing the pilgrimage, agreeing to return the following year.

The Muslims are agitated now. They believe that they have been taken advantage of. Little do they know the final insult still awaits.

When the moment comes to sign the treaty, Suhayl backs away and refuses. When asked what's wrong, he points out that the countersignature line reads "Prophet Muhammad." If he were to sign, by his logic, he would be on record affirming the Prophethood of Muhammad. He haughtily says that this he will not do.

This is too much for the Prophet's companion Umar. Haven't they already come in the weaker position, as pilgrims? Haven't they already given away the store? He stands angrily and is ready to fight.

The Prophet tells him to sit and to acquiesce to the demand. He should remove the words. Umar cannot bring himself to do it. By defying a direct order from his Governor/General/Prophet, he must feel like he is preserving his honor. But honor is not the principal thing on the Prophet's mind. He understands Umar's position, but he knows that there is a higher value at stake.

The Prophet was illiterate, which meant he could not read the treaty himself, and he did not know exactly where—my hands are shaking as I type this—the phrase "Prophet Muhammad" was written. He asked his companions to point out the place, then he took the writing instrument and struck the words himself.

Perhaps the disquiet amongst the Muslims would have grown into an open rebellion if God had not sent down a revelation declaring the moment "a manifest victory."

When the Prophet and his companions return to the Ka'ba to make their agreed-upon visit, the Meccans joined the religion of

Islam in droves. The war was over. The hostility had melted. They begged to join the Prophet's community, and he welcomed them with open arms.[7]

Zayd and Khalil, we live in an age in which people speak of turning tools into weapons. But the deep wisdom of our religion and our country is to do the opposite. I knew a man named Vincent Harding, a hero of the civil rights movement, a champion of young people and nonviolence, who used to say, "I live in a nation that does not yet exist." You never met Uncle Vincent, and he never met you, but you and I and your mom and so many people you love live free in America because of the dream he believed in and the sacrifices he made. You owe him something. He of course never saw it that way. He was just following the path that God had shone a light on. He only loved you and believed in you (he loved and believed in all young people) and knew that you would build that nation of his imagination so that both you and his great-great-grandkids could live in it.

Zayd and Khalil, there are times to come as a warrior, with your fists up, ready for battle. But the lesson of Hudaybiyyah, and of King and Obama and Jane Addams and Uncle Vincent and so many others, is that if you come as a pilgrim and you point to a place where everyone can thrive, people will recognize the strength of your generosity, and they will join you, and we will all win.

ACKNOWLEDGMENTS

T HIS BOOK WENT THROUGH AT LEAST THREE COMPLETE
drafts before finding its way into the final form you hold in your
hands. So many people improved it along the way, including Jennifer
Bailey, Tony Banout, Katie Bringman Baxter, Mary Ellen Giess, Jona-
than Gruber, Amber Hacker, John Inazu, Jeff Pinzino, Paul Raushen-
bush, Carl Robinson, Jennifer Hoos Rothberg, Noah Silverman, and
Teri Simon.

A special thank you to my friend and former student Neil Agar-
wal for not only doing the endnotes but for also offering incisive comments on multiple drafts.

To my editor, Amy Caldwell: I love working with you and Beacon
Press. I appreciate so much your remarkable ability to help me shape
amorphous material into a for-real.

To the board, staff, and network of Interfaith America: thank
you for the space to write this book and the honor of leading the
organization.

To my wife and boys: all love, *all love*.

NOTES

INTRODUCTION

1. *John Lewis: Good Trouble*, dir. Dawn Porter (Magnolia Pictures, 2020), DVD.

2. Ella Baker, "The Black Woman in the Civil Rights Struggle" (address, Institute of the Black World, Atlanta, GA, December 31, 1969), Iowa State University Archives of Women's Political Communication, https://awpc.cattcenter.iastate.edu/2019/08/09/the-black-woman-in-the-civil-rights-struggle-1969.

3. Robert Moses and Charles Cobb Jr., *Radical Equations: Civil Rights from Mississippi to the Algebra Project* (Boston: Beacon Press, 2001), 125.

4. Moses and Cobb, *Radical Equations*, 112.

5. Adam Serwer, "John Lewis Was an American Founder," *Atlantic*, July 18, 2020, https://www.theatlantic.com/ideas/archive/2020/07/how-john-lewis-founded-third-american-republic/614371.

6. Astead Herndon, "Are Racial Attitudes Really Changing? Some Black Activists Are Skeptical," *New York Times*, August 11, 2020, https://www.nytimes.com/2020/08/11/us/politics/black-lives-matter-chicago-roseland.html.

7. Michelle Alexander, "We Are Not the Resistance," *New York Times*, September 21, 2018, https://www.nytimes.com/2018/09/21/opinion/sunday/resistance-kavanaugh-trump-protest.html.

8. See Langston Hughes, "The Negro Speaks of Rivers," in *The Weary Blues* (New York: Knopf, 1926), https://www.poetryfoundation.org/poems/44428/the-negro-speaks-of-rivers; and Vincent Harding, *There Is a River: The Black Struggle for Freedom in America* (New York: Harcourt Brace Jovanovich, 1981).

9. Deepa Iyer, "Mapping Our Roles in Social Change Ecosystems," SolidarityIs and Building Movement Project, 2020, https://buildingmovement.org/wp-content/uploads/2020/06/Final-Mapping-Ecosystem-Guide-CC-BY-NC-SA-4.0-Handles.pdf.

10. Yuval Levin, *A Time to Build: From Family and Community to Congress and the Campus, How Recommitting to Our Institutions Can Revive the American Dream* (New York: Basic, 2020).

11. John Locke, "Second Treatise of Government," originally published 1690, Project Gutenberg, https://www.gutenberg.org/files/7370/7370-h/7370-h.htm.

12. Stacey Abrams, "It's a Privilege to See Yourself Reflected in Leadership," interview by Jake Tapper, *State of the Union*, CNN, November 8, 2020, https://www.cnn.com/videos/politics/2020/11/08/sotu-stacey-abrams-on-kamala-harris-postelex-sot-vpx.cnn.

CHAPTER TWO: BUILDER, CREATING INTERFAITH AMERICA

1. Ani DiFranco, "My I.Q.," track 9 on *Puddle Dive*, Righteous Babe Records, February 1993, compact disc, https://anidifranco.bandcamp.com/track/my-iq-2.

2. Audre Lorde, "The Master's Tools Will Never Dismantle the Master's House," in *Sister Outsider: Essays and Speeches* (Berkeley, CA: Crossing Press, 1984). Originally from remarks given at The Personal and the Political panel, Second Sex Conference, New York, NY, September 29, 1979, https://collectiveliberation.org/wp-content/uploads/2013/01/Lorde_The_Masters_Tools.pdf.

3. Howard Thurman, *Jesus and the Disinherited* (New York: Abington–Cokesbury, 1949). See David Brooks, "A Christian Vision of Social Justice," *New York Times*, March 18, 2021, https://www.nytimes.com/2021/03/18/opinion/social-justice-christianity.html.

4. Peter Salovey, "Free Speech, Personified," *New York Times*, November 26, 2017, https://www.nytimes.com/2017/11/26/opinion/free-speech-yale-civil-rights.html.

5. Muhammad al-Bukhari, *Al-Adab al-Mufrad*, Book 27, Hadith 479.

6. David French, *Divided We Fall: America's Secession Threat and How to Restore Our Nation* (New York: St. Martin's, 2020).

7. Paul Tough, *Whatever It Takes: Geoffrey Canada's Quest to Change Harlem and America* (Boston: Houghton Mifflin Harcourt, 2009).

8. Eboo Patel, "Toward a Field of Interfaith Studies," *Liberal Education* 99, no. 4 (Fall 2013). Originally from remarks delivered at Coca-Cola World Fund Talk, Yale University, January 2013, https://www.aacu.org/publications-research/periodicals/toward-field-interfaith-studies.

9. Samuel Freedman, "A Laboratory for Interfaith Studies in Pennsylvania Dutch Country," *New York Times*, April 2016, https://www.nytimes.com/2016/04/30/us/alaboratory-for-interfaith-studies-in-pennsylvania-dutch-country.html.

10. David Bornstein, *How to Change the World: Social Entrepreneurs and the Power of New Ideas* (New York: Oxford University Press, 2007).

11. Alyssa N. Rockenbach, M. J. Mayhew, M. E. Giess, S. M. Morin, B. A. Staples, and B. P. Correia-Harker, *IDEALS: Bridging Religious Divides Through Higher Education* (Chicago: Interfaith Youth Core, 2020), https://ifyc.org/sites/default/files/IDEALS_report.pdf.

CHAPTER THREE: JEN BAILEY, CRITIC AND BUILDER

1. Jennifer Bailey, *To My Beloveds: Letters on Faith, Race, Loss, and Radical Hope* (Nashville: Chalice, 2021).

2. Jennifer Bailey and Lennon Flowers, "Cultivating Brave Space," interview by Krista Tippett, *On Being*, Public Radio Exchange, October 17, 2019, https://onbeing.org/programs/jennifer-bailey-and-lennon-flowers-an-invitation-to-brave-space.

3. Pádraig Ó Tuama and Marilyn Nelson, "A New Imagination of Prayer," interview by Krista Tippett, *On Being*, Public Radio Exchange, September 6, 2018, https://onbeing.org/programs/padraig-o-tuama-and-marilyn-nelson-a-new-imagination-of-prayer.

4. Toni Cade Bambara, interviewed by Kay Bonetti, in *Conversations with Toni Cade Bambara*, ed. Thabiti Lewis (Jackson: University Press of Mississippi, 2012), 35.

CHAPTER FOUR: CAMPUS AS CRUCIBLE

1. Diaspora Coalition, "DEMANDS: Westlands Sit-In 50 Years of Shame," *Sarah Lawrence Phoenix*, March 11, 2019, http://www.sarahlawrencephoenix.com/campus/2019/3/11/demands-westlands-sit-in-50-years-of-shame.

2. Robert D. Putnam, *Our Kids: The American Dream in Crisis* (New York: Simon & Schuster, 2015).

3. Michael J. Sandel, *The Tyranny of Merit: What's Become of the Common Good?* (New York: Farrar, Straus and Giroux, 2020).

4. Andrew Delbanco, *College: What It Was, Is, and Should Be* (Princeton, NJ: Princeton University Press, 2012), 1.

5. Alasdair MacIntyre, "Reconceiving the University as an Institution and the Lecture as a Genre," in *Three Rival Versions of Moral Enquiry: Encyclopaedia, Genealogy, and Tradition* (Notre Dame: University of Notre Dame Press, 1990).

6. John Courtney Murray, *We Hold These Truths: Catholic Reflections on the American Proposition* (Lanham, MD: Sheed & Ward, 1960), 125, https://www.library.georgetown.edu/woodstock/murray/whtt_c5_1958e.

7. Tara Westover, *Educated: A Memoir* (New York: Random House, 2018).

8. David Brooks, *The Second Mountain: The Quest for a Moral Life* (New York: Random House, 2019).

CHAPTER FIVE: AMERICA, THE PEOPLE'S POTLUCK

1. Andrew Higgins, "In Bosnia, Entrenched Ethnic Divisions Are a Warning to the World," *New York Times*, November 19, 2018, https://www.nytimes.com/2018/11/19/world/europe/mostar-bosnia-ethnic-divisions-nationalism.html.

2. Thomas L. Friedman, "President Trump, Come to Willmar," *New York Times*, May 14, 2019, https://www.nytimes.com/2019/05/14/opinion/trump-willmar-minnesota.html.

3. Diana L. Eck, "What Is Pluralism?" Pluralism Project, Harvard University, 2006, https://pluralism.org/about.

4. Kwame Anthony Appiah, "Nations Are Creatures of Story, Made in the Imagination," talk given at the New School's New Narratives: Immigration and the Peopling of America, Ellis Island, NY, October 6, 2019.

5. Jeffrey Stout, *Democracy and Tradition* (Princeton, NJ: Princeton University Press, 2004), 298.

6. John Courtney Murray, *We Hold These Truths: Catholic Reflections on the American Proposition* (Lanham, MD: Sheed & Ward, 1960), x, https://www.library.georgetown.edu/woodstock/Murray/whtt_index.

7. Eric Klinenberg, *Palaces for the People: How Social Infrastructure Can Help Fight Inequality, Polarization, and the Decline of Civic Life* (New York: Penguin Random House, 2018).

8. Michael Miller, "Immigrant Kids Fill This Town's Schools. Their Bus Driver Is Leading the Backlash," *Washington Post*, September 22, 2019, https://www.washingtonpost.com/local/immigration/immigrant-kids-fill-this-towns-schools-their-bus-driver-resents-the-system-that-brought-them-here/2019/09/22/861c0fb4-d321-11e9-9610-fb56c5522e1c_story.html.

9. Walter Lippmann, *Public Opinion* (New York: Harcourt, Brace, 1922), 25, https://www.google.com/books/edition/Public_Opinion/ZQsaAAAAYAAJ?hl=en&gbpv=1&printsec=frontcover.

10. Marcel Proust, *In Search of Lost Time, Vol. 5: The Prisoner*, trans. C. K. Scott Moncrieff, fourth ed. (New York: Modern Library, 2003). French title À la recherche du temps perdu—*La Prisonnière*, originally published 1923.

11. Robert Putnam, "E Pluribus Unum: Diversity and Community in the 21st Century: The 2006 Johan Skytte Prize Lecture," *Scandinavian Political Studies* 30, no. 2 (June 2007): 137–74.

12. Questlove, "'Mixtape Potluck' Is Inspired by Questlove's 'Food Salon' Dinner Parties," interview by David Greene, *Morning Edition*, National Public Radio, October 24, 2019, https://www.npr.org/2019/10/24/772939228/mixtape-potluck-is-inspired-by-questloves-food-salon-dinner-parties.

13. James Weber Linn, *Jane Addams: A Biography* (Champaign: University of Illinois Press, 2000).

14. Paul Arthur Schlipp, *The Philosophy of John Dewey* (New York: Tudor, 1951).

15. William James, letter to Jane Addams, December 13, 1909, quoted in Louise Knight, *Jane Addams: Spirit in Action* (New York: W. W. Norton, 2010), 158.

16. Walter Isaacson, "The Real Leadership Lessons of Steve Jobs," *Harvard Business Review*, April 2012, https://hbr.org/2012/04/the-real-leadership-lessons-of-steve-jobs.

17. Jane Addams, "Subjective Necessity for Social Settlements," in *Twenty Years at Hull-House* (New York: Macmillan, 1923). Originally from

lecture given in Plymouth, MA, 1892, https://digital.library.upenn.edu
/women/addams/hullhouse/hullhouse.html.

18. Quoted in Jon Meacham, *The Soul of America: The Battle for Our Better Angels* (New York: Random House, 2018). Originally from Jane Addams, *Democracy and Social Ethics* (New York: Macmillan Co., 1902), 10, https://books.googleusercontent.com/books/content?req=AKW5QacIxiQEo T7mM5WylwlM4R-Ax2zL6aM-eqaFUCpU17IIBMGZhKn0BhwT8xdGOljTI _wnQre6kFw-Kny68WZtxExJjtd19WY5z5zKNS77ZddwwoVH4xdav8877FK6w PXAlARAKNITmC-sue40jSIb9eWoGCCJW2TgayGhWo5sgUqEqDzmVnk9 JRv10h1_d8PAu5SUXQn3PLYJk2JDRxSAhY6njxUa5A5IMktjXkp8TPw _kqIMWrof-A2K-4zBIZdSN_ejU77AKbG6qEousvwzR592xzrKDQ.

19. Frederick Buechner, *Wishful Thinking: A Seeker's ABC* (New York: HarperOne, 1993), 118.

CHAPTER SIX: THE OBAMA STORY, THE TRUMP STORY

1. Jeffrey Goldberg, "Unthinkable: 50 Moments That Define an Improbable Presidency," *Atlantic*, January 2019, https://www.theatlantic.com /unthinkable.

2. "End Our National Crisis: The Case Against Donald Trump," editorial, *New York Times*, October 18, 2020, https://www.nytimes.com /interactive/2020/10/16/opinion/donald-trump-worst-president.html.

3. Reporting and fact-checking by Glenn Kessler, Meg Kelly, Salvador Rizzo, and Michelle Ye Hee Lee, *Washington Post*, originally published May 19, 2017, last updated January 21, 2021, https://www.washingtonpost.com /graphics/politics/trump-claims-database. According to the database, the president made 30,573 false or misleading claims in four years.

4. Kelly Wallace and Sandee LaMott, "The Collateral Damage After Students' 'Build a Wall' Chant Goes Viral," CNN, December 2016, https:// www.cnn.com/2016/12/28/health/build-a-wall-viral-video-collateral-damage -middle-school.

5. Zadie Smith, "On Optimism and Despair," *New York Review of Books*, December 2016, https://www.nybooks.com/articles/2016/12/22/on-optimism -and-despair. Originally from remarks given at Welt Literature Prize acceptance, Berlin, November 2016.

6. James Baldwin, "Take Me to the Water," in *No Name in the Street* (New York: Dial, 1972).

7. Salman Rushdie, "Ask Yourself Which Books You Truly Love," *New York Times*, May 24, 2021, https://www.nytimes.com/2021/05/24/opinion /sunday/salman-rushdie-world-literature.html.

8. Jill Lepore, *This America: The Case for the Nation* (New York: Liveright, 2019).

9. Kwame Anthony Appiah, "Nations Are Creatures of Story, Made in the Imagination," talk given at the New School's New Narratives: Immigration and the Peopling of America, Ellis Island, NY, October 6, 2019.

10. Smith, "On Optimism and Despair."

11. Janny Scott, "In 2000, a Streetwise Veteran Schooled a Bold Young Obama," *New York Times*, September 9, 2007, https://www.nytimes.com /2007/09/09/us/politics/09obama.html.

12. Barack Obama, keynote address, 2004 Democratic National Convention, Boston, MA, July 27, 2004, https://www.youtube.com/watch?v =eWynt87PaJo.

13. Barack Obama, first inaugural address, Washington, DC, January 20, 2009, https://www.youtube.com/watch?v=3PuHGKnboNY.

14. Barack Obama, farewell address, Washington, DC, January 10, 2017, https://obamawhitehouse.archives.gov/farewell.

15. Barack Obama, commencement address, University of Notre Dame, South Bend, IN, May 17, 2009, https://time.com/4336922/obama -commencement-speech-transcript-notre-dame.

16. Barack Obama, speech, 2018 Nelson Mandela Annual Lecture, Johannesburg, South Africa, July 17, 2018, https://www.npr.org/2018/07/17 /629862434/transcript-obamas-speech-at-the-2018-nelson-mandela-annual -lecture.

17. Saul D. Alinsky, *Rules for Radicals: A Pragmatic Primer for Realistic Radicals* (New York: Random House, 1971).

18. Obama, speech, 2018 Nelson Mandela Annual Lecture.

CHAPTER SEVEN: THE GENIUS OF RELIGIOUS INSTITUTIONS

1. Jose Mario Bautista Maximiano, "Catholic Church: World's Biggest Charitable Organization," *Inquirer USA*, September 27, 2018, https:// usa.inquirer.net/15692/catholic-church-worlds-biggest-charitable -organization.

2. Robert D. Putnam with Shaylyn Romney Garrett, *The Upswing: How America Came Together a Century Ago and How We Can Do It Again* (New York: Simon & Schuster, 2020).

3. Robert D. Putnam, *Bowling Alone: The Collapse and Revival of American Community* (New York: Simon & Schuster, 2000).

4. Robert D. Putnam and David E. Campbell, *American Grace: How Religion Divides and Unites Us* (New York: Simon & Schuster, 2010).

5. Bob Smietana, "White Christian America Built a Faith-Based Safety Net. What Happens When It's Gone?" *Religion News Service*, October 26, 2020, https://religionnews.com/2020/10/26/white-christian-america-built-a -faith-based-safety-net-what-happens-when-its-gone.

6. See Wilma Rugh Taylor and Norman Thomas Taylor, *This Train Is Bound for Glory: The Story of America's Chapel Cars* (King of Prussia: Judson, 1999), https://www.chapelcarsofamerica.net/online_book.html.

7. Eric Liu, *Become America: Civic Sermons on Love, Responsibility, and Democracy* (Seattle: Sasquatch, 2019).

8. "Aga Khan Development Network: An Ethical Framework," Institute of Ismaili Studies, London, 2000, https://d1zah1nkiby91r.cloudfront.net /s3fs-public/ethical-factsheet.pdf.

9. "Overview of the Aga Khan Development Network," Aga Khan Development Network, June 2016, https://d1zah1nkiby91r.cloudfront.net /s3fs-public/factsheets/AKDN-factsheet.pdf.

10. David Brooks, "A Nation of Weavers," *New York Times*, February 18, 2019, https://www.nytimes.com/2019/02/18/opinion/culture-compassion.html.

11. C. Eric Lincoln and Lawrence H. Mamiya, *The Black Church in the African American Experience* (Durham, NC: Duke University Press, 1990).

12. Barbara Ransby, *Ella Baker and the Black Freedom Movement: A Radical Democratic Vision* (Raleigh: University of North Carolina Press, 2003), https://revolutionarystrategicstudies.files.wordpress.com/2015/12/rs6mjdk.pdf.

13. Ransby, *Ella Baker and the Black Freedom Movement*, 12.

14. Ransby, *Ella Baker and the Black Freedom Movement*, 18.

15. Ransby, *Ella Baker and the Black Freedom Movement*, 50.

16. Charles Marsh, *The Beloved Community: How Faith Shapes Social Justice from the Civil Rights Movement to Today* (New York: Basic Books, 2005).

17. Charles Marsh and John M. Perkins, *Welcoming Justice: God's Movement Toward Beloved Community* (Downers Grove, IL: InterVarsity Press, 2009).

18. Marsh, *The Beloved Community*.

19. Marsh, *The Beloved Community*.

20. Bryan Stevenson, *Just Mercy: A Story of Justice and Redemption* (New York: Spiegel & Grau, 2015). Also see Ezra Klein, "Bryan Stevenson Explains How It Feels to Grow Up Black amid Confederate Monuments," *Vox*, May 24, 2017, https://www.vox.com/2017/5/24/15675606/bryan-stevenson -confederacy-monuments-slavery-ezra-klein.

21. *True Justice: Bryan Stevenson's Fight for Equality*, dir. Peter Kunhardt, George Kunhardt, and Teddy Kunhardt (Kunhardt Films, 2020), YouTube streaming, https://www.youtube.com/watch?v=JfZPl4CFEUc.

22. Ezra Klein, "Bryan Stevenson on How America Can Heal," *Vox*, July 20, 2020, https://www.vox.com/21327742/bryan-stevenson-the-ezra-klein -show-america-slavery-healing-racism-george-floyd-protests.

23. Klein, "Bryan Stevenson on How America Can Heal."

24. From *True Justice*.

CHAPTER EIGHT: THE CHALLENGE OF BEING IN CHARGE

1. *Philly D.A.*, dir. Ted Passon, Yoni Brook, and Nicole Salazar, 2021, Independent Lens, Public Broadcasting Service, streaming, https://www.pbs .org/independentlens/documentaries/philly-da.

2. Frederick Douglass, "West India Emancipation," speech, Canandaigua, NY, August 3, 1857, University of Rochester Frederick Douglass Project, https://rbscp.lib.rochester.edu/4398.

3. *Philly D.A.*, Part 3, https://video.wttw.com/video/part-3-philly-da -episode-3-9lksp7.

4. Ronald A. Crutcher, "Leadership in Crossing Divides," *Inside Higher Ed*, February 19, 2021, https://www.insidehighered.com/views/2021/02/19 /college-president-shares-lessons-learned-navigating-divides-race-class-and -politics.

5. Ibram X. Kendi, *How to Be an Antiracist* (New York: One World, 2019).

CHAPTER NINE: ALIGN THE SUBSTANTIVE AND THE SYMBOLIC

1. Stella Chan and Amanda Jackson, "San Francisco School Board Votes to Rename 44 Schools, Including Abraham Lincoln and George Washington High Schools," CNN, January 27, 2021, https://www.cnn. com/2021/01/27/us/san-francisco-school-name-changes-trnd/index.html.

2. Chan and Jackson, "San Francisco School Board Votes to Rename 44 Schools, Including Abraham Lincoln and George Washington High Schools."

3. Ezra Klein, "California Is Making Liberals Squirm," *New York Times*, February 11, 2021, https://www.nytimes.com/2021/02/11/opinion/california -san-francisco-schools.html. Also see Ross Douthat, "San Francisco Schools, Radicalism and the Pandemic," *New York Times*, January 30, 2021, https://www.nytimes.com/2021/01/30/opinion/san-francisco-school -renaming.html.

4. Alec MacGillis, "The Students Left Behind by Remote Learning," ProPublica, September 28, 2020, https://www.propublica.org/article/the -students-left-behind-by-remote-learning.

5. Daniel Hunter, "5 Pitfalls Black Lives Matter Must Avoid to Maintain Momentum and Achieve Meaningful Change," Waging Nonviolence, July 21, 2020, https://wagingnonviolence.org/2020/07/5-pitfalls-black-lives -matter-must-avoid.

CHAPTER TEN: BE GUIDED BY A VISION FOR,
NOT AN ANGER AGAINST

1. James Baldwin, *The Fire Next Time* (New York: Dial, 1963).

2. Baldwin, *The Fire Next Time*.

CHAPTER ELEVEN: EMBRACE DIVERSITY,
INCLUDING THE DIFFERENCES YOU DON'T LIKE

1. Asma Uddin, *The Politics of Vulnerability: How to Heal Muslim-Christian Relations in a Post-Christian America; Today's Threat to Religion and Religious Freedom* (New York: Pegasus, 2021).

2. Uddin, *The Politics of Vulnerability*, 174–75.

3. Al-Hujurat, 49:13.

4. Uddin, *The Politics of Vulnerability*, 174.

5. Fuṣṣilat, 41:34.

CHAPTER TWELVE: EMBRACE THE MULTIPLE
LANGUAGES OF SOCIAL CHANGE

1. Marc Eliot, *Paul Simon: A Life* (Hoboken: John Wiley & Sons, 2010).

2. Robin Denselow, "Paul Simon's Graceland: The Acclaim and the Outrage," *Guardian*, April 19, 2012, https://www.theguardian.com/music/2012/apr/19/paul-simon-graceland-acclaim-outrage.

3. *Paul Simon: Under African Skies*, dir. Joe Berlinger, 2012; A&E Television Networks.

4. *Paul Simon: Under African Skies*.

CHAPTER THIRTEEN: BE CAREFUL TURNING IDENTITY
CATEGORIES INTO IDEOLOGICAL CATEGORIES

1. J. Edward Moreno, "African American Figures Slam Biden on 'You Ain't Black' Comments," *The Hill*, May 22, 2020, https://thehill.com/homenews/campaign/499214-african-american-figures-slam-biden-on-you-aint-black-comments.

2. *BlacKkKlansman*, dir. Spike Lee (2018; Universal City, CA: Focus Features).

CHAPTER FOURTEEN: SEEK SOLUTIONS, THEN SEEK SCALE

1. Muhammad Yunus, *Banker to the Poor: Micro-Lending and the Battle Against World Poverty* (New York: PublicAffairs, 1999).

CHAPTER FIFTEEN: WELCOME ALL ALLIES

1. Jill Lepore, "Ruth Bader Ginsburg's Unlikely Path to the Supreme Court," *New Yorker*, October 1, 2018, https://www.newyorker.com/magazine/2018/10/08/ruth-bader-ginsburgs-unlikely-path-to-the-supreme-court.

2. David Cole, "Ruth Bader Ginsburg, 1933–2020," *New York Review of Books*, September 20, 2020, https://www.nybooks.com/daily/2020/09/20/ruth-bader-ginsburg-1933-2020.

CHAPTER SIXTEEN: PERSUADE YOUR OPPONENTS

1. Simon Greer and Richard D. Kahlenberg, "Democratic Candidates Can Win by Getting Values Right," *Nation*, February 27, 2020, https://www.thenation.com/article/politics/bobby-kennedy-progressive-values.

2. Kelyn Soong, "How a Black Lives Matter Activist Took the Stage and Got Trump Supporters to Listen at Last Weekend's DC Rally," *Washington Post*, September 20, 2017, https://www.washingtonpost.com/news/inspired-life/wp/2017/09/20/how-a-black-lives-matter-activist-took-the-stage-and-got-trump-supporters-to-listen-at-last-weekends-dc-rally.

CHAPTER SEVENTEEN: CONSIDER CONSTRUCTIVE
ENGAGEMENT BEFORE YOU CANCEL

1. Tara Golshan and Ella Nilse, "Ralph Northam Promised Black Voters a Voice. Will He Listen Now?" *Vox*, February 4, 2019, https://www.vox.com/2019/2/4/18210420/ralph-northam-racist-yearbook-black-voters-resign.

2. Joseph R. Biden Jr. (@JoeBiden), "There is no place for racism in America. Governor Northam has lost all moral authority and should resign immediately, Justin Fairfax is the leader Virginia needs now," Twitter, February 2, 2019, 9:58 a.m., https://twitter.com/JoeBiden/status/1091712355849945088.

3. Astead W. Herndon, "Black Virginians Took Ralph Northam Back. Neither Has Forgotten." *New York Times*, June 14, 2021, https://www.nytimes.com/2021/06/14/us/politics/ralph-northam-virginia.html

4. Herndon, "Black Virginians Took Ralph Northam Back. Neither Has Forgotten."

5. Herndon, "Black Virginians Took Ralph Northam Back. Neither Has Forgotten."

CHAPTER EIGHTEEN: STAND ON THE BALCONY
AND THINK OF A HEDGEHOG

1. Ronald Heifetz, Marty Linsky, and Alexander Grashow, *The Practice of Adaptive Leadership: Tools and Tactics for Changing Your Organization and the World* (Boston: Harvard Business School Publishing, 2009).

2. Jim Collins, *Good to Great: Why Some Companies Make the Leap . . . and Others Don't* (New York: HarperCollins, 2001).

3. Paul Tough, "The Harlem Project," *New York Times*, June 20, 2004, https://www.nytimes.com/2004/06/20/magazine/the-harlem-project.html.

CHAPTER NINETEEN: APPRECIATE THE HISTORY
OF YOUR MOVEMENT, THEN EXTEND IT

1. Kevin M. Schultz, *Tri-Faith America: How Catholics and Jews Held Postwar America to Its Protestant Promise* (London: Oxford University Press, 2011).

CHAPTER TWENTY: BE CAUTIOUS ABOUT BECOMING A SYMBOL

1. Taylor Branch, *Parting the Waters: America in the King Years 1954–1963* (New York: Simon & Schuster, 1988).

2. Bob Dylan, *Chronicles: Volume One* (New York: Simon & Schuster, 2004).

CHAPTER TWENTY-ONE: BE CAUTIOUS ABOUT MAKING
GENERALIZATIONS AND SPEAKING FOR OTHERS

1. Dave Chappelle, "Monologue," *Saturday Night Live*, NBC, November 7, 2020, https://www.nbc.com/saturday-night-live/video/dave-chappelle-standup-monologue/4262843.

2. Courtney Martin, "To Those Calling for Unity," Examined Family, November 11, 2020, https://courtney.substack.com/p/to-those-calling-for -unity.

3. Marjorie Rhodes, "How Generic Language Leads Children to Develop Social Stereotypes," *Huffington Post*, August 7, 2012, https://www .huffpost.com/entry/generic-language-social-stereotypes_b_1753667.

4. Matthew Yglesias, "The Great Awokening," *Vox*, April 1, 2019, https://www.vox.com/2019/3/22/18259865/great-awokening-white-liberals -race-polling-trump-2020.

5. Zach Goldberg, "America's White Saviors," *Tablet*, June 5, 2019, https://www.tabletmag.com/sections/news/articles/americas-white-saviors.

6. Thomas Edsall, "The Democratic Party Is Actually Three Parties," *New York Times*, July 24, 2019, https://www.nytimes.com/2019/07/24 /opinion/2020-progressive-candidates.html.

7. Kwame Anthony Appiah, "Go Ahead, Speak for Yourself," *New York Times*, August 10, 2018, https://www.nytimes.com/2018/08/10/opinion /sunday/speak-for-yourself.html.

CHAPTER TWENTY-TWO: BE CAUTIOUS ABOUT THE SINGLE STORY

1. Chimamanda Ngozi Adichie, "The Danger of a Single Story," July 2009, TEDGlobal, Oxford, UK, 18:33, https://www.ted.com/talks /chimamanda_ngozi_adichie_the_danger_of_a_single_story.

2. Elijah Megginson, "When I Applied to College, I Didn't Want to 'Sell My Pain,'" *New York Times*, May 9, 2021, https://www.nytimes.com /2021/05/09/opinion/college-admissions-essays-trauma.html.

3. Trabian Shorters, "'You Can't Lift People Up by Putting Them Down': How to Talk About Tough Issues of Race, Poverty, and More," *Chronicle of Philanthropy*, June 26, 2019, https://www.philanthropy.com /article/you-cant-lift-people-up-by-putting-them-down-how-to-talk-about -tough-issues-of-race-poverty-and-more.

4. Kwame Anthony Appiah, *The Lies That Bind: Rethinking Identity* (New York: Liveright, 2018).

5. Next Narrative for Black America, https://nextnarrative.net.

CHAPTER TWENTY-THREE: BE CAUTIOUS ABOUT
THE FALSE SOCIAL MAP

1. Luis Noe-Bustamante, Lauren Mora, and Mark Hugo Lopez, "About One-in-Four U.S. Hispanics Have Heard of Latinx, but Just 3% Use It," Pew Research Center, August 11, 2020, https://www.pewresearch.org/hispanic /2020/08/11/about-one-in-four-u-s-hispanics-have-heard-of-latinx-but-just -3-use-it.

2. Musa al-Gharbi, "White Men Swung to Biden. Trump Made Gains with Black and Latino Voters. Why?" *Guardian*, November 14, 2020, https:// www.theguardian.com/commentisfree/2020/nov/14/joe-biden-trump-black

-latino-republicans; Leila Fadel, "How Did President Trump Appeal to Voters of Color?" NPR News Las Vegas, NPR, November 5, 2020, https://www.wxxinews.org/post/how-did-president-trump-appeal-voters-color.

3. Marlon Marshall et al., "2020 Post Election Analysis: May 2021," Third Way, June 7, 2021, https://www.thirdway.org/report/2020-post-election-analysis.

4. Zack Stanton, "How 2020 Killed Off Democrats' Demographic Hopes," Q&A with David Shor, *Politico*, November 12, 2020, https://www.politico.com/news/magazine/2020/11/12/2020-election-analysis-democrats-future-david-shor-interview-436334.

CHAPTER TWENTY-FOUR: BE CAUTIOUS WHEN ACCUSING OTHERS

1. Michael Powell, "Inside a Battle Over Race, Class and Power at Smith College," *New York Times*, February 24, 2021, https://www.nytimes.com/2021/02/24/us/smith-college-race.html.

2. Anne Applebaum, "The New Puritans," *Atlantic*, August 31, 2021, https://www.theatlantic.com/magazine/archive/2021/10/new-puritans-mob-justice-canceled/619818.

CONCLUSION

1. Taylor Branch, *The King Years: Historic Moments in the Civil Rights Movement* (New York: Simon & Schuster, 2013).

2. T. S. Eliot, "Tradition and the Individual Talent," *The Egoist*, September 1919.

3. Nike, "Dream Crazy," advertisement narrated by Colin Kaepernick, 2018, available on YouTube, https://www.youtube.com/watch?v=jBnseji3tBk.

4. Kerry James Marshall, *Mastry*, exhibition, Metropolitan Museum of Art, New York, October 2016–January 2017, https://www.metmuseum.org/exhibitions/listings/2016/kerry-james-marshall.

5. Lisa Desjardins, "How Mayor-Elect Lori Lightfoot Plans to Address Chicago's Gun Violence 'Epidemic,'" *PBS News Hour*, April 3, 2019, https://www.pbs.org/newshour/show/how-mayor-elect-lori-lightfoot-plans-to-address-chicagos-gun-violence-epidemic.

6. Mos Def, "Fear Not of Man," track 1, *Black on Both Sides*, Rawkus and Priority Records, October 1999, compact disc.

7. Karen Armstrong, *Muhammad: A Prophet for Our Time* (New York: HarperCollins, 2006).

INDEX